TWAYNE'S WORLD AUTHORS SERIES

A Survey of the World's Literature

Sylvia E. Bowman, Indiana University

GENERAL EDITOR

SOUTH AFRICA

Joseph Jones, University of Texas

EDITOR

Pauline Smith

(TWAS 80)

TWAYNE'S WORLD AUTHORS SERIES (TWAS)

The purpose of TWAS is to survey the major writers—novelists, dramatists, historians, poets, philosophers, and critics—of the nations of the world. Among the national literatures covered are those of Australia, Canada, China, Eastern Europe, France, Germany, Greece, India, Italy, Japan, Latin America, New Zealand, Poland, Russia, Scandinavia, Spain, and the African nations, as well as Hebrew, Yiddish, and Latin Classical literatures. This survey is complemented by Twayne's United States Authors Series and English Authors Series.

The intent of each volume in these series is to present a critical-analytical study of the works of the writer; to include biographical and historical material that may be necessary for understanding, appreciation, and critical appraisal of the writer; and to present all material in clear, concise English—but not to vitiate the scholarly content of the work by doing so.

Pauline Smith

By GEOFFREY HARESNAPE

University of Cape Town

Twayne Publishers, Inc.　　::　　New York

For My Mother and Father

Preface

Pauline Smith's creative work had to be a close reflection of her experience of life. She confesses she could only write what she *felt* and *knew* to be true. As a result, the people and places influencing her talent become of great importance. I have tried to sketch in an impression of the Little Karoo, which forms the background to so many of her stories, and to outline briefly her relationships with the two dominant men in her writing life—her father, Dr. Henry Smith, and her friend and literary "master," Arnold Bennett.

She was a painstaking writer, and her work was often interrupted by ill-health or arrested by self-doubts. Her published books are few. Although she had contributed a number of sketches and verses under a pen name to Scottish newspapers before she met Bennett, it was not until she had known his encouragement that she gained the confidence to find her own distinctive voice. During her long life, however, she wrote many diaries and letters. There are also other writings (articles, a play, miscellaneous fragments, etc.) among her literary remains. From this quite extensive supporting material I have made a small selection for treatment in this book. In particular, I have chosen one journal which shows how closely her fiction was based upon stories she was told and characters whom she met on a tour of the Little Karoo area in 1913–14.

Most of Pauline Smith's adult years were spent away from the country of her birth and the austere landscape which she loved. Why did she feel this strong need to write about a small section of South Africa? It had something to do, it seems, with recollections of a more than usually happy childhood which coincided with the years before her father's sudden and unexpected death. She began by setting down memories for her own consolation;

and, by degrees, the Little Karoo and its people became vehicles for expressing a vision essentially poetic. An effort has been made to point out the presence of this poetry, to discuss its associated symbolism, and generally to evaluate her most significant work.

Pauline wrote about the rural Afrikaners of an isolated community. Critics have commented appreciatively on how her English dialogue somehow gives an impression of spoken Afrikaans. Some biographical details have been presented which help to show what her knowledge of this language was, and suggestions have been made as to how she achieved this particular speech effect. Bearing in mind those readers who are unacquainted with the details of South African life, I have also tried to fill in a more general background here.

Reading *The Beadle* or *The Little Karoo* immediately brings to mind the work of Olive Schreiner whose imaginative evocation of the Karoo and its lonely people won admiration round about the turn of the century and still excites attention. The writings of Herman Charles Bosman and Uys Krige, both of whom have at times described the rural Afrikaner, are also relevant. At the invitation of the producers of this Series, I have compared these authors briefly with Pauline Smith. The book ends with a selection of responses to her work from some modern South African writers. Their particular points differ widely, but they are at one in recognizing a genuine and lasting talent.

I am very grateful to Professor Joseph Jones for the opportunity of developing in book form what had begun some years ago as postgraduate research. My thanks go to the Council of Witwatersrand University for a Research Grant which helped me in the preparation of the manuscript. I am grateful to the Council of the University of Cape Town for permission to quote from Pauline Smith's correspondence, her journal, "The Last Voyage" and "The Cart"; also to the Council of the University of Cape Town and Jonathan Cape Ltd., for permission to quote from *The Little Karoo, The Beadle, Platkops Children* and *A.B. . . . 'a minor marginal note.'* An acknowledgment is due to A. Balkema Ltd., for quotations from the South African edition of *The Beadle*.

Finally, warm thanks to my wife, Lesley, for listening and criticizing so helpfully while the work was being done.

Cape Town   G. L. H.

Contents

Contents

Chronology

1883	Pauline Urmson Smith was born in Oudtshoorn, Cape Province, South Africa, on April 2.
1895	She was taken to Britain and to boarding school by her father, Dr. Henry Urmson Smith.
1902	Began to contribute sketches and verse under a pen name to Scottish newspapers.
1905	She journeyed to South Africa. Kept a diary from January to June.
1909	Pauline met Arnold Bennett in a small hotel near Vevey, Switzerland.
1910	Contributed to *The Evening Gazette*, under a second pen name, Janet Urmson. Spent part of the year with Bennett and his wife in their cottage at Fontainebleau.
1913	She set out to South Africa for a nine-month tour. Compiled a journal and gained ideas for her short stories and novel.
1914	Returned to England.
1925	Eight short stories appeared in the first edition of *The Little Karoo*.
1926	Publication of *The Beadle*. Came out to South Africa. Kept customary journal.
1927	Returned to England.
1930	Reissue of *The Little Karoo* with addition of "Desolation" and "The Father."
1931	Death of Bennett.
1933	Publication of *A.B. . . . 'a minor marginal note.'*
1934	Journeyed to South Africa.
1935	Publication of *Platkops Children*.
1959	Pauline Smith died in England on January 29.

CHAPTER 1

Oudtshoorn and Europe

ABOUT thirty miles inland from the little Cape Province settlement of George and over the Outeniqua Mountains, lies the town of Oudtshoorn. At the beginning of this century it expanded rapidly with the growth of the ostrich-feather trade. Today it is still an important agricultural and military centre. When one drives up from George via the new Outeniqua Pass, one can at times look down onto the tortuous windings of the old Montagu Pass road. In the old days, ox wagons would creak their way down, inching round the corners with wheels locked, while barefooted Coloured boys screwed the brake handles at the rear. Ascending would be an even greater strain. The oxen would heave at the yokes and stumble onto their breasts, while the driver's whip crashed in the air above their horns.

Nowadays, by car, it is easy to climb up from the coastal forests where the giant trees contort themselves in their struggle for the light, and to cross the peaks to the clear air and startlingly red earth of the next plain. This great, meandering land trench bounded by two parallel ranges of mountains is known as the Little Karoo. Where there is water, the soil is amazingly fertile. Valleys green with lucern or fruit trees finger their way into the foothills of the stony ranges. Whitewashed houses stand in groves of pepper trees, their steep, thatched roofs built for coolness beneath the searing sun.

The greatest impression is of vast dryness and heat. Dawns and dusks are splendid in crimson and vibrating violet. Sometimes the sunset is like beaten gold along the horizon. At night the stars burn intensely white. One could expect a Pharaoh to want to raise a pyramid here; or one would be able to imagine it as the kind of land to which Abraham was drawn when he left the city of Ur in his search for the hidden God.

The farmers and *bywoners* (poor farm tenants and sometimes labourers) who live here are comparatively isolated. Of necessity they are thrown back on their own resources, with plenty of time to contemplate. Among the most remote the order of life is unchanging and conservative, in many ways similar to the world of the Old Testament and the exact opposite to the anthill life of modern cities.

Oudtshoorn itself is changing. The ways of the South African cities, Cape Town and Johannesburg, are being felt there. In the High Street, cheek-by-jowl with the old stone Dutch Reformed Church, are cheap restaurants, all chromium and blare. Along the back streets, however, where the houses are shuttered and cool in their gardens of fruit trees, one gains an impression of what the town was like eighty years ago—when Pauline Smith lived there with her family. All is silent in the noon heat. Only the faintest gurgle of water comes from the irrigation furrows in the plots. This world of Oudtshoorn and the Little Karoo provided the imaginative impulse for a novel and a series of short stories by a woman whose whole existence was coloured and enthralled by the place where she was born and where she spent the first few years of her life.

Pauline Smith was born in Oudtshoorn on April 2, 1883. Her father, Dr. Henry Urmson Smith, had come to South Africa for the sake of his health and was the first properly qualified medical practitioner in that village, then not yet forty years old. Her mother, Miss Jessie Milne before her marriage, came from Scotland where she had trained as a nurse.

The first twelve years of Pauline's life were full of vivid, unforgettable experiences. She spent many happy hours playing in the large garden of her father's house with her sister, Dorothy, her cousin, Wilfred, and young friend, Colin, the son of the chemist who dispensed for her father. Sometimes Dr. Smith would take her on his journeys to the outlying districts when he made professional calls on the farmers and their families. Pauline would observe carefully the way they spoke, the operation of their slow, certain thoughts, their dress and their homes.

This important, formative period was to end—very suddenly. When Pauline Smith was twelve years old, her father took her to Britain and to boarding school. In a letter, Dr. Killie Campbell, an old friend of hers, recounted an anecdote which shows her great heartbreak at leaving South Africa. The story goes that when she was being carried off in a Cape cart, she jumped off and ran back to her house, sobbing, and beating against the door with her fists. Almost immediately after arriving in Britain, her father died. In one blow Pauline Smith was bereft of the country she had grown to love and the man whom she had constantly looked up to, depended on, and admired.

Dr. Henry Urmson Smith had made an impression on Oudtshoorn. He seems to have been a man of energy, humour, and common sense, with a quick sympathy for and understanding of others. At one time he was elected mayor of the town, and he founded the first Choral Society there. The doctor also had a way with children. He was severe, yet he could always remember and understand the world of a child's imagination. He had been especially appreciative of his sensitive young daughter, and now that he was dead, she missed him intensely. In *A.B. . . . 'a minor marginal note'* she writes:

. . . ill health which had been my lot since childhood, and the shock of my father's sudden and early death, from which, though years had passed, I had never fully recovered, had made me in all things diffident and despondent.[1]

Not only was he gone. The world of Oudtshoorn and the Little Karoo, which meant so much to her, was 6,000 miles over the sea. In "Why and How I became an Author," an article written in her later years, she writes:

Much too, I owe, to the unconscious storing up in my memory, through those impressionable years, of all that was dear and familiar to me, as well as that which was mysterious and strange, in the small world—set in a wide, sun-parched plain, bounded north, south, east and west by mountain ranges—which made my universe.[2]

And again in *A.B. . . . 'a minor marginal note'*:

All my happiest memories and my most formative impressions were those of my South African childhood and my father's companionship.[3]

Perhaps her love for her father and her love for the place were connected in some mysterious way. Possibly if she had not lost her father she would not have brooded so intently on the Little Karoo. The fact remains that to comfort herself with memories of those happier days she began, slowly, and desperately unsure of herself, to write. From these early efforts emerged the sketches which were to be published many years later under the title of *Platkops Children.*

This early writing was accomplished with many misgivings. Pauline Smith was entirely on her own, without literary friends or guides. Her reading had been sporadic, directionless, and limited. She writes of her childhood in South Africa:

It did not even make me, so far as I can remember, particularly bookish, for books in quantity played no part in the out-of-door life we led as children in our small Dutch village in the Little Karoo. But for that very reason, perhaps, such books as we did read made a tremendous impression upon me. Among these were *Rab and his friends,* the tales of Mrs. Ewing, *Robinson Crusoe,* and the amazing and terrifying *Fairchild Family.* But the three which influenced me most deeply, though I was then too young to realize their beauty as literature, were, the Old Testament, "The Ancient Mariner," and "The Vicar of Wakefield."[4]

Despite her limited experience, she moved on from the South African sketches to write others of Scottish village life. Some of these were published in Scottish newspapers. Always she wrote slowly and while suffering from ill-health. She began to fear that authorship was something beyond her. But finally, with patience, she began to write a novel.

Pauline Smith had written about one-third of this novel when she met a man who was to have a profound influence on the rest of her literary life. In 1909, she had travelled with her mother to spend a holiday at a small hotel in the hills above Vevey in Switzerland. Here, by some ordinance of fate, she came to know Arnold Bennett, the English novelist and short story writer, who at that time was beginning to establish a wide reputation with the publication of *The Old Wives' Tale.* Bennett took what writing she had produced, read it instantly, and summoned the trembling young woman to his private rooms. It is easy to imagine her, nervous and delicate, sitting forward on her chair, perhaps twisting and untwisting her handkerchief in her lap, while the "master" rested back in his chair to discourse at length.

After tea, while his wife sat and sewed, he lit a cigarette and told me bluntly that "anybody" could have written the Scottish sketches (which had found publication): that not everybody could have written the children's stories (which had never been published): and that though if I finished my novel a publisher would probably be found for it, the artist in me (having achieved the children's stories) must know just how bad the novel was.[5]

Pauline Smith took his advice. Of this early writing only *Platkops Children* is now to be found in book form. It seems she never tried to reprint the Scottish sketches. As for the novel, her own instincts immediately recognised the justice of Bennett's criticism.

His damning of those opening chapters gave me a confidence in his judgment which no praise could have won, and brought me so overwhelming a sense of relief and release that it was as if he had broken down for me an imprisoning wall and drawn me out into the open air. I destroyed my novel and never afterwards regretted it.[6]

Arnold Bennett was confident that the young woman had powers which could be developed. He invited her to spend part of the following year with him and his wife in their cottage at Fontainebleau. Here he began systematically to educate her. He introduced her to modern novels—English, French, and Russian. In her own words, she was "drawn to a hill-top where keen airs blew through new worlds of thought that were mine for the taking."[7] Not only did Bennett help her with reading. Many an evening, when he had completed a whole day's writing, he would insist that she read aloud to him what she had written, and he would criticise and instruct. She had begun to work "with a clearer purpose for this self-appointed master,"[8] but the difficulties and the bitterness of spirit in which she created her stories remained the same. At Fontainebleau she started on a second novel.

The next spring, when she travelled to Italy with the Bennetts and settled with them in Florence, she was still working on her new manuscript. Again the self-doubts and the pain with which she wrote asserted themselves.

Everything I tried to write here was futile—and well and bitterly I knew it. . . . It was in one of these despairing moments that I asked him if I had not better give up writing altogether, for I could not, it seemed to me, with all my work as bad as it now appeared, have any talent deserving of his interest.[9]

Arnold Bennett's reaction was to give her a good scolding. He said he knew she had the talent; otherwise he would not be wasting his time on her. He could not, however, buoy up her fading spirits and health. Soon after she fell seriously ill with an onset of quinsy. This was followed by a yet more serious attack. The Bennetts had to leave her in the Casa di Cura of the Blue Nuns in Florence when they returned to England. It was in Italy that she destroyed her second attempt at a novel. When she had recovered she returned to England.

Pauline Smith had now lived through her teens, her early, middle, and late twenties. She was just turning thirty and had not yet produced any of the work which Arnold Bennett felt she was capable of writing. Ill-health, self-doubts, and a painful introspection had made her development slow and difficult.

In July 1913, she set out for Cape Town to spend nine months staying on farms in the Little Karoo and travelling in the Western Cape. This time, described briefly in "Why and How I became an Author" as "a year spent among our old friends in the Little Karoo,"[10] was of the greatest importance in stimulating and forming her mature work.

Arnold Bennett still had unwavering confidence that she would be a writer when she left for South Africa on that momentous trip. He advised her to make a journal of her impressions during her stay which she could use later for her creative writing. This she did, and a full account of that visit can be read in what I call her *South African Journal*, over six hundred pages of typescript full of information and delight for anyone interested in the genesis of *The Little Karoo* short stories and *The Beadle*.

In this journal one reads of a Pauline Smith, still young and very gentle, travelling out from Oudtshoorn to the farms Mill

River and Vlakteplatz in the Little Karoo, then crossing the
Outeniqua Mountains and visiting Mossel Bay, George, Knysna,
and the Wilderness. She records stories told her, describes
characters she had met, especially the poor *bywoners* in whom
she was much interested. Often there are entries mentioning that
she had gone down with sickness; for even in the healthy climate
of the Little Karoo she was dogged by poor health. From time to
time, especially important stories or characters appear. These
are later to be transmuted by her imagination, to form the plots
and people of her short stories and her novel. Sometimes the
original anecdotes are detailed, very like the imaginative story
created from them. Occasionally, as in the celebrated short story,
"The Pain," she has taken just a hint and created a plot around it.
For *The Beadle* she has taken two actual farms and fused them
together into an imaginative one. There is a profusion of source
material in this journal. In Chapter 9 the reader may examine a
few relevant extracts and compare them with the story and
novel finally created.

When Pauline Smith returned to England in May 1914, her
childhood memories of the Little Karoo had been immeasurably
strengthened by her new experiences. New characters and situations filled her mind, just waiting to be included in her writing.
As a girl, she had been lured by the mystery and isolation of the
place. In her own words:

In those unhustled days, when a visit to the nearest neighbouring
village meant a day's journey by cart or several days' journey by ox-
wagon "over the mountains," the Dutch farmers, among whom my
father's work as a doctor lay, still lived in a primitive simplicity close
to their God. Among these people we had many friends and all their
way of life and their slow, brooding talk which fell so naturally in
translation into the English of the Old Testament, was full of interest
to us. Often my father took us with him when he visited their farms
and these journeys with him across the wide empty veld; the long low
white-washed homesteads we came to—some bare and treeless and
poor as they were bare, some set in green lands in narrow fertile
valleys among the mountain foot-hills: the mountains themselves,
varying always in colour, over which, once a year, we travelled to the
sea: the long quiet village its streets lined with giant eucalyptus trees,
poplars and willows, to which we returned from all our wanderings

with such deep content—all these things were beautiful to me as a child.[11]

Now, in her mature years, she had returned to the very same people, country, and farms. As a result, everything she saw and noted, from an adult's point of view now and with an adult's notions of character and important detail, was invested with a moving and mysterious significance. Her childhood inspiration and her adult impressions working together had at last prepared her for her first spell of mature writing.

CHAPTER 2

Mature Writing and Later Years

W HEN PAULINE SMITH returned to England in 1914, she began slowly, and with the accustomed attacks of illness and pain, to write the short stories which were to appear in *The Little Karoo* sequence published by Jonathan Cape in 1925. Arnold Bennett was always near, inspiring her with his confidence, jaunty and persistent. At this time she was writing with little hope of publication. Both she and Bennett believed that no editor would be happy to take short stories so uniformly tragic as those of *The Little Karoo*. The older writer had approached several.

Unfortunately, Pauline could write no others until she had got what was at hand out of her system. She sent six stories—"The Schoolmaster," "The Sinner," "Anna's Marriage," "The Pastor's Daughter," "Ludovitje," and "The Sisters"—to her self-appointed "master." All of these, the first six she wrote, won his approval and were put back into her drawer.

Arnold Bennett was worried. Something was lacking in his protégée's work. It was not until she sent the seventh story, "The Miller," to him that he realised what it was. In his opinion her stories needed a more definite geographical setting, greater local colour, so that the reader in England would be able to get a better hold of them. In *A.B. . . . 'a minor marginal note'* she records how he realised that "from the British public's point of view my stuff was simply suspended in the air. There was no path up to it and no key to its enigmas."[1]

Later, when she started on her eighth short story, "The Pain," she tried to put it into a more specific and closely described setting. When Arnold Bennett saw this story completed, he immediately set about finding someone to print it. "The Pain" was the first of her mature work to be published and found its way into the pages of *The Adelphi,* then edited by John Middleton Murry. In February 1925, almost eleven years after she had returned from South Africa, Jonathan Cape published these eight short stories in a volume entitled *The Little Karoo.* The book must have been unexpectedly popular, for it went into a second, a third, and a fourth impression in March, April, and December of the same year. "The Pain," written last of the eight, was placed first in the collection.

Now Bennett, ever ebullient and badgering, began to insist that she start the novel which, he felt convinced, it was in her to write. For some time there had lain in her mind, together with *The Little Karoo* stories, a tale which proved to be too large for the short-story form whenever she tried to write it. It is clear to any reader of *The Little Karoo* and *The Beadle* that these two books have a common setting and way of life for their inspiration. Andries Lombard, the sick and morose miller in the short story of that name, appears again in *The Beadle.* The novel and the short story have the same setting. The *nagmaal,* or Dutch Reformed communion service, forms a high point in both.

The Beadle was Pauline Smith's third attempt to write a novel, and, as is to be expected, it came slowly, with much pain. She writes:

> Never, it seemed to me, did what I wrote do justice to my people as I saw them, and never, in spite of A.'s satisfaction with each portion in turn, would I be able to bring the whole to completion. Even his amazed and oft-repeated "But if I believe in you, why can't you believe in yourself?" could not rid me of my sense of failure and foreboding. Ill-health may have added to my diffidence, for my work was frequently stopped by illness, and once again throat trouble drove me into hospital and was followed by a slow and despondent convalescence.[2]

She was gripped by the work. Her imagination had taken control of her with a terrible, demonic power. At one stage in the writing a doctor advised her to stop for fear that its "hold" upon her should kill her. At last it was completed and published by Jonathan Cape in 1926. With the publication of *The Beadle* she reached the end of her first spell of literary creation, twelve years of hard and painful effort. This was the time of her greatest output and the most ambitious of her work.

In October 1926—now forty-three years old—she came out to South Africa for another visit. We know that Pauline once again kept a diarised account of her experiences. Clearly, she was still practising the methods of observation by which she had gained material for *The Little Karoo* and *The Beadle*. Miss Marie Stegmann, an old friend of Pauline Smith in Oudtshoorn, mentions in a letter how close certain descriptions in the short story "Desolation" are to events which actually happened when the authoress was visiting South Africa. The following is an extract:

I may mention that in one of the stories in *The Little Karoo* ("Desolation") she describes the trek of an old woman and boy with their little flock of sheep and goats. That was taken from something she saw in the Karoo on her way to visit my sister in the Beaufort West district. That part of the district might well be called the Verlatenheid, and her description on pages 174 and 175 is absolutely correct, almost photographic.

In 1927 Pauline Smith returned to England and immediately began work on the long short story called "Desolation." This, like all her other work, was written "very slowly, and through much unreasonable misery."[3] By this time her grasp of writing short stories was such that Arnold Bennett had no criticisms to make. She writes in *A.B. . . . 'a minor marginal note'* that this story perhaps moved him more than all the others.

Soon after this, possibly in 1928, she wrote, "knowing nothing of the technique of the theatre, and at times appalled by my own presumption,"[4] a one-act play called "The Last Voyage." This play is set in Cape Town and seems markedly inferior to the short stories and novel set in the Oudtshoorn district. The comparative weakness of this work is another suggestion of the close association between the Little Karoo and the powerful working of Pauline Smith's imagination. Here she is only 300 miles away from Oudtshoorn and her artistic power is already losing its grip "The Last Voyage" did not satisfy Arnold Bennett, and it is probably for this reason that she did not, as far as can be ascertained, ever attempt to have it produced.

[21]

The next short story she wrote was set again in the Little Karoo and called "The Father." Both this short story and "Desolation" were added to *The Little Karoo* volume when it was reissued by Jonathan Cape for "The Travellers' Library" series in 1930. There are no hints for either "Desolation" or "The Father" in the *South African Journal* she kept on her 1913-14 trip. Therefore it seems reasonable to suppose that the impressions for both were gained on her 1926 visit.

Together with the typescript journal in the care of the Library of the University of Cape Town, is another short story, "The Cart," which Pauline Smith does not include among those referred to in *A.B. . . . 'a minor marginal note.'* Clearly it was inspired by her 1913-14 trip to South Africa, since the idea for it can be seen recorded in the *South African Journal*. It was published in *The Cape Argus* on December 19th, 1925.

"The Cart" is in part comical, reflecting the cumbersome practical humor of its Afrikaans characters. Certain touches in its characterisation remind one of her handling of Jan Beyers and Tan' Linda de Neysen in *The Beadle*. This intrusion of humour would suggest that it was written after *The Little Karoo* series as we know it, when Pauline Smith had expelled the sombre clouds of her more tragic vision, and when she was preparing for the greater variety of tone, ranging from comedy to intense sadness, in *The Beadle*.

Pauline Smith was forty-eight when the man who had been for her a dynamo of strength and optimism died after a short illness. With Arnold Bennett's death in 1931, she seems to have lost the inspiration and support to encourage her in further artistic effort. It must always be remembered that she never wrote with great facility; her imagination was not powerful and flexible enough to turn to a great variety of new topics. For a long time she had been troubled with ill-health and had virtually retired to a country life in a cottage in Dorset. Now, without "A.B." to back her up, her self-doubts seem to have mastered her, and she spent most of the remaining twenty-six years of her life living with her sister, Dorothy, away from the literary world and the whirl of the big cities.

In 1933, Jonathan Cape published *A.B. . . . 'a minor marginal note,'* which provides such a fund of information about Pauline

Smith's own life, and which is her tribute to the writer who had done so much for her own career. This book is the only considerable work which she achieved without Bennett's help and chivvying. At such a time her memories of him were strong and poignant enough to overcome the hesitation and pain which inevitably beset her when she put pen to paper. Her sketches of the novelist in his varying moods are sympathetic and evocative. One has a vivid picture of Bennett staggering stubbornly around the deck of his steam yacht, the *Marie Marguerite,* when all his guests had been reduced to helpless sea-sickness on a stormy crossing from Falmouth to Guernsey.

> For twenty-eight hours that tempestuous crossing had lasted, and through all its miseries there had loomed from time to time the stern apparition of A., clad in thick Jaeger garments, bearing in a souptureen the mess of shredded meat which he insisted, regardless of protest or consequence, should be eaten while he waited.[5]

Or one may see him in a quieter spot, sitting on the nursery floor in his house at Cadogan Square, engaged in grim opposition of wills with his daughter.

Years before, Pauline Smith had started *Platkops Children* to set down for her own comfort a record of a surer and lovelier life as she had known it. A.B. . . . *'a minor marginal note'* was possibly written "to set down for her own comfort" memories of a man whose friendship had meant warmth and security for her. The book contains the same sympathetic portrayal of character, awareness of detail and measured clearness of style which can be found in *The Little Karoo* and *The Beadle.*

One other book remained to be published. When Pauline Smith came out to South Africa in 1913-14, she had taken the *Platkops Children* sketches, which Arnold Bennett had admired, to Maskew Miller, a publishing house in Cape Town. There is no record in the *South African Catalogue of Books* of 1941 that this was ever printed by them. It was not until 1935 that the book was published by Jonathan Cape, just about thirty years after the sketches had been written.

After 1933, Pauline Smith does not appear to have written very much other than letters. In the University of Cape Town library there are the article "Why and How I became an Author" and some reminiscences of the Scottish writer, William Alexander. During the later years of her life, however, she did make other journeys to South Africa. Fortunately some of her more informative letters from these times are extant. They show that she was in Swellendam, an old Afrikaner village in the Cape Province, in October 1937. She writes to her friend, Dr. Killie Campbell, in Durban:

My dear Killie,
    You see I am back in Africa again and am very glad to be here! At the moment my sister and I are in a lovely little thatched cottage which has been lent to us by a preacher. It lies on a slope of the foothills of the Swellendam mountain . . . [our?] simple needs are supplied by an adjoining farm . . .

    From dates on other letters it is clear that Pauline Smith was in South Africa in April, September, and October 1934, April, May, June, July, August, October, and November 1935, and in February and May 1936. She also visited the country from October to December 1937 and probably stayed on into the following year, for there is a solitary letter dated March 1938. Parts of these visits were spent in Oudtshoorn and on the surrounding farms, the places she had used with such strength in her writing. But she also went further afield, to the Eastern Cape, the Transvaal and Natal.

    It seems that, as she grew older, it became increasingly difficult to make the long sea-voyage from England to South Africa, an undertaking which even in her young days had left her ill and dispirited. In a letter from Dorset to Dr. Killie Campbell, dated January 1952, Pauline Smith—then sixty-nine—writes:

    I wish so much I could come out once again to see you all, dear Killie. I fear now I may never be able to do so. I do not grow stronger as I grow older, alas!

    Despite her almost constant ill-health, Pauline Smith was a painstaking and dedicated artist. She needed Arnold Bennett to urge her on, but often her artistic judgment both of her own work and his was more thorough and genuine than his impressions and snap decisions. In *A.B. . . . 'a minor marginal note'* she records how her "self-appointed master" often undervalued the brilliance of his best works just as he overrated and dogmatically supported things which did no justice to his talent. She was afraid of his descending into what she calls his "impressionable second-best."[6] Of her own work she writes:

In life I had neither his courage nor his honesty in the stating and facing and accepting of facts, but in my work I could get down nothing which I did not "see," or, often painfully, feel and know to be true. I could not make situations to suit the needs of a story as a story—all I could do was to describe, often after a long waiting, that slow development in the lives of my characters which lay outside my will.[7]

Pauline Smith drew heavily on her own life and experience for her work. The fortitude and patience which can be seen in many of her characters are her own. The slow pace and isolated setting of her stories is repeated in the slow, long, and quiet life which she lived, away from the cities, the new trends and flurries of the twentieth century. The sympathy and clear sight with which she views her fictional characters was employed when it came to her friends. From her letters one can see that she is often concerned about the health of others, enters into their predicaments, is profusely thankful for favours and acts of friendship.

Miss Marie Stegmann of Oudtshoorn speaks of her as an unusual, sensitive, and kindly person. Although she was dogged by ill-health, she remained considerate. Dr. Killie Campbell writes in a letter:

I have many memories of Pauline, but the dominant one is of her constant pain. Her neuralgia gave her no rest, and although an operation on the nerve was suggested, she would not consider it. During the war we began sending her food parcels, but she wrote and asked us not to continue, as there were so many others who needed them more. She was indeed a very wonderful person.

While Pauline was living in seclusion, her published writings became better known. Just under a year before her death on

January 29, 1959, she was presented with an illuminated scroll signed by twenty-five South African writers. Part of the inscription read: "We South African writers in English and Afrikaans have felt moved to join our names together in offering you a tribute of our admiration."

CHAPTER 3

Pauline Smith and Arnold Bennett

I T HAS been shown briefly how Arnold Bennett helped Pauline Smith with her writing and how important a place he came to take in her life and friendships. When they first met at Vevey in Switzerland she was twenty-five and he forty-two or forty-three. In order to understand why he took so well to her and why she responded so fully to his masterful and often paternal manner, one has to go back to her childhood in Oudtshoorn when she was a sensitive, shy girl, encouraged and made secure by her father's understanding and care. Miss Marie Stegmann of Oudtshoorn, who knew Dr. Henry Smith, remembers him as an unusual and striking character. She recounts that Pauline was deeply attached to her father. As a child her one wish was that she could have a beard like him.

This attachment can be seen both in her earlier writings and in *A.B.* . . . '*a minor marginal note.*' In fact, in the article "Why and How I became an Author" she herself confesses to that hankering after the beard! Once one knows that *Platkops Children* is thinly disguised biography and autobiography, the sketches which that book contains become great sources of information about Pauline Smith's early feelings. Her father's deep imprint is found in this writing.

She suggests here that he had been an exceptional man who had understood children. Somehow he had the ability to look back over the years and see into the minds and imaginations of young boys and girls; he knew what approach to take to thrill them and entice their interest. It was he who told Pauline and her sister, Dorothy, that Queen Victoria was coming to spend the night with them, and that she had her axe and crown in the box on the horse-cart[1]—thus getting them into a quiver of excitement.

In the sketch "Paoli in England" Pauline Smith describes how, as a child, she was given a beautiful bustle dress when she went overseas with her mother. She wanted to know what would happen when she died and became an angel. Where would her wings fit in the bustle dress? None of her relations in Britain could answer that. So she had to wait until she returned to South Africa before her father, with his unique talent for understanding children, could solve her problem. As soon as he knew it, he exclaimed, "What, little daughter! Did none of them know there's an angel a dressmaker in heaven with a pair of scissors?"[2]

Although he understood his children's ways and thoughts, this remarkable Dr. Smith could also be severe. In "Aunt Jane's Weddin'" Pauline Smith relates how her father admonished her and her sister after they had been naughty one day.

An' that night at supper our father said, all of a sudden, like he always does, If ever I hear little girls walking on factory walls like jackals, I beat.

An' we said Oh, father!

An' he said again, And if ever I hear of little girls throwing stones from an upstairs window I send them to boarding-school.

An' we said, Oh, father! an' got off our chairs in a mos' tremenjous hurry an' climbed on his knee.[3]

In A.B. . . . 'a minor marginal note' Pauline Smith mentions many characteristics of Arnold Bennett which she admired. One of the first of his qualities was his practicality and common-sense, "that ruthless Midlands downrightness which, so alarming and discouraging to others, was in my own case to lead to the enduring friendship set down for remembrance here."[4] Bennett was practical and resourceful not only in his business affairs, but also in his writing and criticism of art and literature. Pauline Smith writes:

In later years I never went with him to any play or art collection without being . . . enriched either by the down-right Five-Towns common sense of his criticism, or by the companionship—I know no

other way of expressing it—into which one was drawn by his own response to beauty when he found it.[5]

The English novelist was always definite, ever self-assured. In his masterly and practical manner she almost certainly found an echo of the character of her father, who had always insisted on simplicity and directness both in writing and in conducting the affairs of life. She relates with thankfulness how Arnold Bennett took control of all her literary business. It was he who posted off her first short stories to editors. Later he would draft letters on her behalf, precise and dispassionate in their statement of terms. When she protested in alarm to what she considered to be some especially exorbitant demand, he would firmly impress on her the commercial value of her work. He was a successful businessman, wasn't he? Well then, she must be patient and abide by his methods. With a strange, tender irony she looks at the boyish zeal of the man who assumed automatically that she was in no way capable of handling her own affairs.

In the first years of their friendship Arnold Bennett took Pauline Smith very definitely under his wing. It has been related how he invited her to Fontainebleau and later to Florence. Yet, when, on the face of it, she had failed as a writer with the destruction of her second attempt at a novel, he never lost interest or withheld from her the appellation of "fellow artist." He was to help her in many practical ways for the rest of his life. He had begun to widen her reading at Fontainebleau, and after that he never really stopped. In *A.B. . . . 'a minor marginal note'* she recounts how, on one occasion, she mentioned that it was difficult to get books in her seclusion in Dorset. Arnold Bennett got to his feet saying "That must be seen to,"[6] and at once fetched a pile of books from his own shelves. From then on he posted batches of new books to her at regular intervals.

When it came to her own writing he proved himself a relentless critic and taskmaster. "Whenever and wherever we met it was always my work that was A's. first subject of concern,"[7] she writes. One has a telling and intimate picture of their different characters and of the mixture of outright affection and "master and disciple" in their relationship in a scene where Pauline Smith describes

Bennett's reaction to the half-written manuscript of "The Pain" which she had posted to him in despair.

> After dinner, in his study, he produced my Ms. his verdict upon which I had not dared to ask, and circling round the table like an excited schoolboy, waving the manuscript above his head, stammered triumphantly *"Now* you've done it! Now . . . you've done it . . . And I . . . have shown you . . . *how to do it!"* His delight and satisfaction, and my own relief, brought me suddenly close to tears—and as suddenly his mood changed. "Now," he said firmly, *"you go home and finish it."*[8]

In other parts of *A.B.* . . . *'a minor marginal note'* one reads of Pauline Smith and her "master" wandering round the streets of London while they discuss the plot of her play, or sitting in the swaying "Lovat Fraser" saloon of the steam yacht *Marie Marguerite* while he insistently, ruthlessly goes through the plot and characters of *The Beadle* point by point.

With his practicality and his readiness to give a lead, Arnold Bennett was like Pauline Smith's father. There were other ways in which the novelist resembled Dr. Smith. Describing the way in which he treated his daughter, Pauline writes: "I saw in him again, as long ago I had seen it, that Victorian severity founded upon justice which I had known in my childhood."[9] Reading this, one is at once reminded of Dr. Smith as he is depicted in *Platkops Children,* promising to beat the little daughters who had walked like jackals on factory walls. Also, one can sense from these sketches that the doctor must, in his way, have had a creative imagination—an ability to enter sympathetically into the minds of others, while at the same time remaining disinterested, seeing issues in proper, logical perspective. It is precisely this ability for which Pauline commends Arnold Bennett:

> He was, in fact, one of those rare beings who not only recognises but respects the right of another to hold his own opinion and to make his own mistakes.[10]

The "strange mixture of sympathetic understanding and almost ruthless detachment"[11] in his character was what established his value in her eyes. And this perhaps was the most important

quality, because it was the most rare, shared by Arnold Bennett and Dr. Smith.

It would not be right to say that Arnold Bennett was purely a substitute for Pauline Smith's father. Undoubtedly this is an important part of their relationship. His paternal attitude is apparent in a hundred instances; her daughter-like reactions are as clear. But in *A.B. . . . 'a minor marginal note'* there are certain things she writes and remembers about him which do not fit easily into the kind of reminiscences to be expected from one who was a protégée pure and simple. With the stern and rigorous truthfulness which she applies to the characters in her writings, she regards Bennett's smaller vanities. When she stayed with him and his wife at Fontainebleau she mentions that he had designed various devices for the orderly running of the cottage. "And he was masculinely convinced that none but himself could manage the stove in the hall, the *salamandre* in the *salon* and the geyser in the bathroom."[12] Here is a picture of the novelist, slightly ridiculous in his egotism, and yet with that childlike zeal and simplicity women sometimes discern in men. In this description is sympathy, an appreciation of and yearning towards the stupid one, admiring him for the very vanity which is exposed.

This is even more clear in another passage from *A.B. . . . 'a minor marginal note.'* Pauline Smith realises that in public he liked

to be known by his upstanding tuft of hair: to be famed for his fob and for the cut of his clothes—which, however elegant, he wore always a little stiffly: to have his assured place in a First Night audience, though he slept through many a First Night . . . to be in the know as to the best-but-not-yet-famous restaurants in Soho.[13]

Here she is listing many of his faults and vanities, but she knows them well and seems to describe them with a certain affection and pride. As in the previous passage, there is joy in thinking about and a yearning towards the self-assured man with his comical upstanding tuft of hair. She is interested enough to notice that he wears his clothes a little stiffly. This is not the way in which she would have understood and described her father.

A wife is sometimes known to love her husband for the very

idiosyncrasy with which the man at times annoys and upsets her. Love enables a person to understand the vanities and short-comings of another very clearly, yet at the same time to value him or her because or in spite of those things. And when, as in these descriptions, there is an exposure of weaknesses and a joy in the man who has them, there must be, in some form or other, love. Pauline's love for Arnold Bennett was of a very distant and accepting kind. It hovered always on that indistinct borderland where friendship ends and love begins. Bennett was very much older, and similarities between him and her dead father estab-lished that line of their relationship very strongly. She was always a little overawed by him. Besides, he was married, and it was in her nature to accept this prior claim completely. If she had been aware of his attraction for her she would have turned her thoughts in another direction at once. She writes: "I had, and could have, no place in his world, nor he in mine."[14]

In Pauline's own life can be discerned something which she infuses into the characters of Andrina in *The Beadle* and Niccoline Johanna in the short story called "The Pastor's Daughter." When Henry Nind wants to leave the farm Harmonie, Andrina, who has been his lover, surprises him by putting up no fuss. It is his will and he must go back to his own world if he wants to, is her reasoning. Who is she to hold him there? Pauline practised this kind of self-effacement herself. She is also like the austere, re-signed Niccoline Johanna who was never able to marry Paul Marais, but who was able, through acceptance, to win through to a sweet serenity of mind.

Certainly her friendship with Arnold Bennett deepened as time went by. "Our friendship . . . was like some tree of quiet steady growth whose shade and shelter, for me at least, increased with every year,"[15] she writes in the section of *A.B. . . . 'a minor marginal note'* called "In Later Years." In those later years she did not see him very often, yet they corresponded regularly. The un-derstanding between them must have been full and rich; for just before Bennett caught the chill in France which was to lead to a recurring form of influenza and, later, to his death, she seemed to have a premonition that the end was near. The feeling arose from a fairly trivial incident. In a letter she had com-plained about the weather as an excuse for not working. He

had replied, telling her that was rubbish. She must light a fire and a lamp and forget it. For her it was a strangely beautiful day when she received his reply. She felt peaceful and fulfilled, thinking of the long years of friendship lying behind the note on her desk. It was then that on an impulse she picked up her pen to write to him of what their relationship had meant to her.

So deeply and so strangely did this sense of fulfilment move me, so clearly was the moment impressed upon my mind as marking for ever for me the realisation of something beautiful and complete, that when at last I took up my pen and wrote "I am rebuked about the weather—but no heat of fire and no light of lamp bring me such warmth and radiance as do your letters, and after twenty-two years of friendship I say it," it was as if I did so both for remembrance and in farewell.[16]

This was indeed a moment of strong intuition. Sometime afterwards Arnold Bennett died. Like Niccoline Johanna she was left alone with her patience and her resignation. And, apart from *A.B. . . . 'a minor marginal note,'* one has no knowledge of what she felt or thought in the long, subsequent years.

CHAPTER 4

Platkops Children

PAULINE SMITH describes *Platkops Children* as "some children's stories which were in fact memories of my own South African childhood."[1] They were written very early, before she had met Arnold Bennett and received from him the education and impetus to make possible her later work. Nevertheless, many qualities and characteristics which are peculiar to her writing can be seen here for the first time. The talent, which was later trained to the writing of adult stories, is abundant in these sketches.

It is important to realise how close the incidents recounted here are to events in Pauline's own childhood. The four children described in this book as Pato, the Paoli one, Six, and Nickum D seem actually to have played in a big garden on Dr. Smith's Oudtshoorn *erf* round about the 1890's. According to Miss Stegmann of Oudtshoorn, who was able to identify them easily, Pato is Dorothy, Pauline's sister (later Mrs. Webster); Six is Colin Hicks, the son of the man who was Dr. Smith's dispensing chemist; Nickum is Colonel Wilfred Smith, Pauline's cousin; and the Paoli one is Pauline herself.

Playing together almost every day, these children enjoyed a sunny and active life. They are always looking around them with the fresh sight of childhood, and the authoress takes pains to convey the way in which they regard people and things. She is especially anxious to show how a child feels the reality of the objects around him with a lyrical intensity. There is splendour, vividness and mystery in his vision, as if he were living in a dream. In the first sketch there is a description of Six's father.

Sis's father, they say we mus' insplain, has the Surgery with the great big gold and blue bottles in the window, an' a very nice

Surgery man inside who sometimes gives us thin round little gela-
tine lozenges to suck out of a jar, an' lights magnesium wire for us.[2]

This is related from the children's point of view. The things
which count with them are the two great bottles filled with alluring liquids, the lozenges, which they can describe minutely, and
the burning magnesium. All these are sense impressions, brilliant
and mysterious. Here the chief importance of the surgery man
is that he supplies the sweets and lights the wire. Take Jubilee
Time in Platkops Dorp:

You know when it was Jooblee time there were flags an' magic-
lantuns everywhere, an' a great crowd in the markit place, an' a big
table, an' our father on the top of it speakin' to the people, an' the
people cheerin' like anythin'.[3]

Once more the children see the event from their viewpoint. They
do not understand, nor do they worry about, the reason for the
assembly or the decorated town. They have not realised that it
is because their father is a civic leader that he is up on the table
making a speech. For the girls it "jes' shows what a great man
our father is."[4] On the other hand the colours, the excitement
and the movement speak to them with a simple and sensuous
intensity.

Pauline Smith has another method of conveying the children's
way of looking at the world. She uses a type of description which
lists objects of interest to them almost categorically. In "The
Perlite English Boy," Pato, Paoli, Six, and Nickum take Perceval
Gordon-Gordon, the boy from England, around their garden.

We took him firs' to the proper garden that has geranium hedges
an' myrtle hedges, an' sugar-birds nests, an' banksia roses everywhere
an' wistaria an' borganvilia an' lilac as well. . . . An' we took him
to the orchard on one side of the lawn, where there are apples, an'
pears an' plums an' apricots an' peaches an' punkins. An' then we
took him across the lawn where the almond trees are an' the passion-
flower summer-house where the nest is that a snake lives in . . . then
we took him to the next orchard where there are pomegranits and
quinces and grapes for hedges, an' peaches an' apricots an' nectrins
an' watermelons an' figs an' termaters. An' he didn' say anythin'.[5]

The long list of fruits, shrubs, flowers, and trees tends to overwhelm the reader and gives him an inkling of how life is for the children when all these things crowd in upon their sensitive awareness. In the phonetic spellings, Pauline Smith tries to capture the way the children spoke of these things. She wants to show that the "pomegranits," the "nectrins" and the "termaters" were upon their tongues, parts of their everyday life. After Perceval Gordon-Gordon has been shown round the garden he has all the talk knocked out of him, despite his velvet suit and his leather gloves. Like the Platkops children, he has fallen beneath the mysterious spell set up by this multitude of created objects. He too has been drawn into this child's Eden.

Occasionally the children's way of describing may be very funny. They show that they misunderstand the real point of what is going on. In "The Queen" Dr. Smith is working in his study, apparently examining some medical specimens through a magnifying glass. The children report it as follows:

An our father was lookin' at thin's through a glass. An' they were little long splashes with spots on them. An' there was a pink one.
An' we said, Oh father, what is this?
An' he said. Chat-a-man's—eye.
An' there was a yellow one. An' we said, Oh father, an' what is this?
An' he said. Chat-a-man's—eye.
An' Six said, Goodness grayshus, what man ever had eyes like that, he'd like to know?[6]

Another example occurs after the children have gone to the wedding of their Aunt Jane and Uncle James.

An' at the honeymoon a mos' incitin' thin' happened to our new uncle James an' aunt Jane. An' it was this. They were outspanned up in the mountains, sittin' by the side of a blackberry bush talkin' mos' intrustingly about their new upstairs, when all of a sudden an' ole cow came along.[7]

The exciting thing for the children was that the cow tossed both of them into that blackberry bush. And that they should be

talking "most intrustingly" about the upstairs floor of their house
in their first moments alone together! This is certainly the children's point of view not that of the lovers!

Platkops Children is a blend of humour, lyrical description,
and pathos. Readers who have come to know Pauline Smith
through *The Little Karoo* short stories are often surprised to
hear that she was able to make people burst into happy laughter.
If the joking and surprising incongruities in *Platkops Children*
were to be submerged beneath her more tragic vision in *The
Little Karoo*, the laughs come back in the short story called "The
Cart," parts of *The Beadle*, and in certain passages of *A.B. . . . 'a
minor marginal note.'* When we take all of Pauline Smith's work
into consideration, we shall see that her view of life was not one-
sided. Realism, poetic descriptions, severity, tears, and laughter
all find their place at some stage or other in her art.

The men and women who are presented in *Platkops Children*
are seen purely through the eyes of the children, sometimes in
an incongruous perspective. Pato, Paoli, Six, and Nickum D have
a simple and direct way of describing them, and sweep away the
subtleties and hypocrisies with which grownups confuse the real
images of themselves and their motives. Paoli says of her father.

Our father you know is a very great man indeed. He jes' says
'Come' an' you come, an' 'Hook it' an' you hook it like that man in
the Bible, an' everybody calls him 'Dokter.'[8]

Although the girls do not understand why the doctor has authority over the other people of the town, they recognise it as
it applies to themselves. He reminds them of the Roman centurion
they have heard about in their Bible stories. They do not appreciate the meaning of his profession. The mere fact that others
call him doctor shows that he must be great.

Other people are kind, especially if they like children and look
after them well—like Ou-Pa and Ou-ma Carel on the farm. A few
are seen, clearly and unblinkingly, in their selfishness and cruelty,
like Red Nose, the Balloon Man's assistant, and the man with the
whip who was slashing at Somersaults and his horse in the circus
ring. Finally there is Katisje, the girls' Coloured nannie, who is

responsible in so many ways for moulding their characters. She consoles them when their baby brother dies and fills their imaginations with stories of the veld.

The adult reading *Platkops Children* has the double enjoyment of seeing an incident clearly described from the children's point of view and, at the same time, of appreciating the real state of affairs. An outstanding example of this is the verse called "Spook Abram." Pato and Paoli are intrigued by the Coloured man who often bobs up in the garden outside their nursery at nighttime. Katisje, their nannie, tells them that he is a ghost, or *spook*, in this way carefully hiding the fact that he is one of her boy-friends. If they talk about him to their parents or anyone else, "Spook Abram" will take them away to Kama's valley, where the devil lives. But, they ask, if Abram is a *spook*, how can Katisje go walking with him in the mealie land? Ah, she says, when a *spook* comes calling for you, you must go; otherwise you will die. This verse is beautifully handled, conveying the weird joyful imaginings of the children, and the double meaning is held right through to the concluding stanza.

There are seven poems in this book. They are supplementary to the prose sketches and help to expand the picture we have of Paoli's childhood. Two of them ("Trinka's House" and "The Jackal") recount stories told to her by her nannie, Katisje. Four of the others are written in a semidramatic form and contain dialogue. Not all of the seven are effective. In occasional stanzas, Pauline Smith's efforts to create the colloquial English spoken in the Little Karoo break down, when a too-educated phrase or expression is introduced. In the poem "Fruit Drying" we read

> Dinka's brought her piccanin,
> Dill the coffee-kettle,
> Light has brought her lapje-pop,
> Time it takes to settle![9]

The last line is out of keeping. The phrase is too homely and comes from the wrong social class to be effective in this poem about the Coloured workers, or *volkies,* of Platkops Dorp. "Katisje's Patchwork Dress" contains a stanza in which the old nannie's speech is twisted into improbability by the demands of a rhyme.

> "An' dis? Yo' Pa give me dis flag
> To show how I be loyal
> At Jooblee time—look here's de Queen
> An' all her Fam'ly Royal."[10]

Pauline has better success in re-creating the Little Karoo style of English in the prose sketches. One ought not to forget that this is an important part of her art. With the Little Karoo fixed indelibly as it was in her memory and imagination, it is quite understandable that she should try to reproduce the language as well as the colours, the characters, and the atmosphere of that place. As she always looked back in later life to those happy days of childhood, she seems also to have adhered to the way of speaking she first learned. A South African poet, Mr. Roy Macnab, related on a visit to the University of Cape Town that when he went to visit Pauline at her Dorset home just before her death, he was surprised to hear that she still had a pronounced Little Karoo accent.

It is this Karoo accent, together with the usual distortions in children's pronunciations, which is conveyed through the mouths of Pato, Paoli, Six, and Nickum D in this book. The language they use differs from standard English in the pronunciation of individual words, in the use of unusual phrases or standard phrases in different contexts, and in the introduction and influence of Afrikaans words. Notable among the words different in pronunciation are *droinin room* for drawing-room, *instronnery* for extraordinary, *perlite* for polite, *sich* for such, *jes'* for just, *lantuns* for lanterns, *pianner* for piano, *intrusting'* for interesting, *instremely* for extremely, *tremenjously* for tremendously, *pertickler* for particular. Some of these changes are due mainly to child pronunciations. Others show the influence of Afrikaans upon English in that district; for example *droinin' room* and *jes'*. Among the phrases in unusual contexts is *goodness grayshus*. This becomes an exclamation used with special emphasis and great frequency. Others are *a mos' tremenjous* (as in *a mos' tremenjous long prayer*), *instremely intrusted* (i.e., extremely interested), and *mos' pertickler*. Afrikaans has intruded itself so naturally into her South African English that she has to give a glossary at the end of *Platkops Children,* a list of forty-four words ranging from exclamations of surprise such as *Allamachta* and *Alle-wêreld* to everyday terms like *lapje* (rag) and *Kerkraad* (church council). When Six jeers at Aidie Kanneymeyer, who is on his way to fetch his violin, his strange, half-sung, rhythmical taunt—*Aidie-ka-Paidie Kar-rix-tix-taidie*—could have been used by any Afrikaans child.

If one considers Pauline Smith's work as a whole, one notices that there are many themes, incidents, and descriptions which appear more than once. The authoress wrote from her own experience, drawing upon what had moved or touched her. *Platkops Children* stands near the beginning of her writing and contains descriptions and incidents which will take their place amongst the finest parts of her later work.

The sketch "Ou-Pa Carel's" shows that Pauline Smith's childhood provided part of the inspiration for the stories in *The Little Karoo* and for *The Beadle*. In this chapter Pauline writes that "a little black girl stood behin' our father's chair wavin' the flies away with a cow's tail."[11] Many years later, when Pauline visited the farm Vlakteplatz in the Uniondale District on her South African tour of 1913, she mentions that "a little Coloured girl walked round and round waving . . . a branch instead of the old cowtail to keep off the flies."[12] Other descriptions of the farmhouse, and the Schoemanns who owned it, help to identify the farm to which Pato and Paoli went as Vlakteplatz. This farm and Mill River in the Langkloof Valley seem to be the principal ingredients for the farm Harmonie which Pauline Smith has created for some of *The Little Karoo* short stories and for *The Beadle*.

While Pato and Paoli were playing hide-and-seek with little Ludovic at Vlakteplatz, they went into Ou-pa and Ouma's bedroom where they thought he might be hiding. From under the bed they pulled a big black box, finding to their horror that it was a coffin. Ou-ma comes into the room and tries to comfort them.

An' Ou-ma Carel said Allamachta! again, an' put Pato down on the floor an' pulled the lid of the coffin off. An' there was nothin' in it but some white thin's an' a smell a camfer an' a big black shawl.[13]

She tries to convince them that the box was kept just for storing linen, but the Paoli one (Pauline) knew "that whatever Ou-ma an' Pato said it was really Ou-pa's coffin waitin' for him."[14] A long time later Pauline Smith is to create the character of Ou-ma van der Merwe, the warm and loving old lady in *The Beadle,* who "had in readiness . . . both her shroud and her coffin and the shroud and coffin of her 'man.' "[15] It is quite possible that the coffin which Pauline Smith saw as a child inspired the description in *The Beadle.* Moreover, the big black shawl which she saw in it surely becomes the black cashmere shawl in which Mevrouw van der Merwe wraps her dead Harmonie neighbours when they go out to be buried. Alida, the name which is given to Ou-ma Carel's daughter in *Platkops Children,* is used for the Ou-ma herself in *The Beadle.*

On the way to Ou-pa Carel's, the Paoli one describes a scene which filled her with joy:

we came to the top of a very steep kopje, an' there between us an' the nex' one was the river. An' oh, but it is beautiful! With tremenjous great red rocks goin' high up in the sky, an' wild white geese flyin' about among them, an' the river far away down below.[16]

Later, when Pauline Smith was writing the short story called "The Schoolmaster," the joy, the vision, and the scene came back to her. Then she wrote:

The banks of the river here are steep, and on the far side are the great red rocks that give the drift its name. Here the wild bees make their honey, and the white wild geese have their home. And that day how beautiful in the still clear air were the great red rocks against the blue sky, and how beautiful against the rocks were the white wings of the wild geese.[17]

A comparison of the two descriptions shows how deeply ingrained those childhood impressions must have been.

"Ludovitje," a short story in *The Little Karoo,* which describes the death of a young boy, is heavy with grief and emptiness. Yet, somehow, the despair is turned into a strange sweetness by the authoress's intuitions of the mystery of things and Ludovitje's parents' belief in a transcendent life. Pauline Smith possibly gained the power to write this story by the sad experience of her baby brother's death. This is recorded in the sketch "Jackie" in

Platkops Children. The poem, "The Comforting Ayah," contains the sweet sadness afterwards to appear in the short story.

Pauline Smith's habit of returning in her writing to things which had touched her imagination can be seen in this final and vivid example. In *Platkops Children* she describes Paoli's (i.e., her own) visit to Britain. Here she met a Scottish writer, William Alexander; and the girl and the elderly man took to each other at once. In later life when she was writing a short article on that writer, she mentions several of the incidents already recorded in *Platkops Children*, including her fascinated admiration for the water which gushed from the taps in his house.

This collection of childhood sketches deals then with the district and the people from which and from whom will spring the imaginative world of Harmonie, the Aangenaam Valley, and the Magerplatz. Pauline creates the impression of a lyrical, mysterious, and vivid world seen through the eye of childhood. However realistic and sombre she becomes in her later writings, the Little Karoo will remain a place vividly imagined, presented with an intensity which is more than the everyday.

An important theme which runs through her writing is that harmony and peace of mind can come to a person when he lives in close accord with nature. His isolation drives him to a full awareness of the mystery of things and even to a knowledge of God. This idea occurs early in *Platkops Children* in two poems, "Trinka's House" and "The Jackal."

> Trinka's house stands all alone,
> Alone in Trinka's garden:
> Trinka's garden's sand and stone
> And veld until its mountain.
>
> Trinka's house is made of reeds,
> Made of reeds and rushes:
> Trinka's house is thatched with weeds,
> Thatched with weeds and bushes.[18]

Trinka, this unknown, unimportant person, lives in a house which is built entirely of natural things. The poem goes on to say that she has no carpets, chairs, or tables. There is nothing artificial or manufactured in her house. And Trinka is alone. Her house stands by itself. Her garden is austere—sand and stone—until it merges with the empty veld and the stark, open mountains of the Little Karoo. These descriptions also have symbolic value, telling us of Trinka's asceticism, solitude, and acceptance. She takes without dissatisfaction what nature gives her. Her reward is a life of peace and oneness with nature.

> Trinka's lamp's the bright full moon,
> The stars they are her candles:[19]

The woman's life is lighted by the heavens. Her bed "is silver sand,"[20] . . . the silver suggesting that it is precious to her. The reader guesses that she has a special knowledge of God, and Pauline Smith confirms this feeling in the last stanza:

> Trinka's cup's a calabash,
> A calabash—God grew it
> In the veld for Trinka's house:
> God and Trinka knew it.[21]

"Trinka's House" is not an outstanding poem. There are certain jingling rhymes and trite lines which are disappointing when read aloud. On the other hand, the poem condenses in its symbolism and simple story the idea that a person may be elevated spiritually by living an isolated, impoverished, and simple life. This is why Pauline is interested in her poor *bywoners*, the farm-labourers working long hours on another man's farm, barely keeping themselves in food and clothes.

In "The Pain" Juriaan and Deltje van Royen are like Trinka in their simplicity and solitude. They live in a lonely house in the mountains above the Aangenaam Valley; and they are rich in joy and faith. In "Desolation" the old *bywoner* woman, Alie van Staden, has learned acceptance and many virtues through poverty. Aalst Vlokman, the proud, self-righteous beadle of the Harmonie church, learns acceptance and the mystery of things only when he has been forced by his own confession to leave his position in the community and to go wandering in search of his daughter.

"The Jackal" tries to convey Pauline's idea of the mystery of nature, its power and arbitrariness.

> I wonder what that jackal wants
> Away out on the hill,[22]

Paoli wonders as she lies in bed. Katisje, the Coloured nannie, tells her that she has seen the jackal's home in Kama's Kloof, near the graveyard. As the jackal is mysterious, so is he associated with the mystery of death:

> . . . he creeps at night
> Along the low mud wall,
> And tries to count the tombstones there
> That stand so straight and tall.[23]

This jackal comes to see if the Paoli one is safe in bed.

> And rolls his eyes, Katisje says
> And nods and nods his head.[24]

Here the jackal is like a phantasm. Its action is unearthly. The animal has become the principle of mystery itself, a mystery which penetrates to and understands the inmost thoughts of the girls lying in their beds.

> And then that golden jackal goes,
> Sniff-sniffing round and round,
> Away to Kama's Kloof again
> And never makes a sound.[25]

Except for his eerie cries, we cannot know where he is. He is silent in his movements because he is mystery and cannot be fathomed. More important, he has become a golden jackal, a rich creature of the imagination, above everyday life and invested with wonder. If the children are good, Katisje says, the jackal is happy. But if they are bad he weeps and will come outside their bedroom at night.

> To look at us in bed,
> And roll his eyes like 'Tisje says
> And nod and nod his head.[26]

He has become one with the mystery of conscience. This vision of the great jackal rolling his eyes and nodding his head is omi-

nous and admonitory. Again the poem as a whole is not excep-
tionally good. Lines like "It's really really true"[27] and "Just everything we do"[28] are sugary and unreal baby talk. However, as in
the case of "Trinka's House," the poem encloses in convenient
symbolism and a simple story an imaginative intuition presented
more powerfully and less obviously in later work. An example
occurs in "The Sinner." The weak *bywoner*, Niklaas Dampers,
is oppressed whenever he is alone in the quiet, mysterious fields.
He thinks of God and feels that his inmost thoughts are being
examined. He can never be one with the world around him until
his conscience has been set at rest.

In many ways *Platkops Children* sets the pattern for Pauline
Smith's later work. Incidents and characters which interest her
later are presented here for the first time. The girl Paoli is already
showing that her imaginative interest is confined to the Little
Karoo area. The sketch "How Paoli went to Cape Town" describes the city:

. . . only streets an' houses an' a south-easter, an' people who don't
know you walkin' about in it, an' not worth writin' about in our
book.[29]

This exclusive interest is certainly true of the older Pauline Smith.
Her *South African Journal* and her one-act play, "The Last Voyage," show that when she is away from the Little Karoo her
imaginative powers fade and the colour goes out of her work.
Most of the interesting entries in her journal were made when
she was staying either at Oudtshoorn or in the surrounding district. "The Last Voyage," which is set in Cape Town, is among
the more feeble of her creative writings. For some strange reason
her powers to create are bound up with the place and district of
her birth.

In *Platkops Children* Pauline already shows the ability to think
in terms of a larger canvas. The book is carefully constructed to
form an imaginative whole. Each sketch is not an independent
thing, but relates to the others. In one of the poems we may get
some information which throws light on the narrative ten or
twenty pages before. This book shows that Pauline Smith is already a conscious artist. Her style is clear, faithful to fact,

ordered, and well-proportioned. In her handling of characters, like Ou-pa Carel and Katisje, she shows the deep sympathy and impartiality which are among the most telling qualities in her later work. She has begun to grapple with the problems of rendering unusual and distinctly flavoured dialogue.

One of her greatest beliefs—that the value and meaning of life come from experience and a patient acceptance of one's condition —is implicit in this book. This notion is given an image in the concluding poem, "Katisje's Patchwork Dress," where each patch in the old nannie's dress recalls some bitter or joyful experience in her life. As a series of sketches *Platkops Children* is charming and the Karoo English dialogue is well done. But compared to her later writings it shows itself to be a little parochial. It was not until she had been introduced to other writers and other ways of life that she was able to see her beloved Little Karoo in the more meaningful perspective of her mature work.

CHAPTER 5

The Little Karoo—The First Eight

THIS chapter deals with eight stories which appeared in the first edition of *The Little Karoo* published in 1925 by Jonathan Cape.

I *"The Pain"*

Pauline Smith had written seven of *The Little Karoo* stories before she started "The Pain." When Arnold Bennett read the first part of the manuscript, he was confident that it had the definite setting which the earlier tales had lacked. Here was a story whose realism was invested with a strange blend of sadness and joy, and it was in a powerfully described place.

Juriaan and Deltje van Royen are a simple old couple of the *bywoner* class. For nearly fifty years they have lived in an isolated part of the mountains, hiring a stretch of land from the owner of the local farm. They have been poor, they have no children—yet they have been content, accepting their lot as the will of God. Like Trinka's house of the poem in *Platkops Children* theirs is humble and close to nature. The walls are of mud, the floors a mixture of cow-dung and ashes. The single window has no glass.

Now, at seventy, Deltje has contracted a mysterious pain. Juriaan goes to Harmonie to fetch "Grandmother's Drops" from the Jew-woman's store. But now even the drops, which they have believed in implicitly, are no longer effective. Once more at the Harmonie store, Juriaan hears that at Platkops dorp there is a new hospital where men and women may be healed of all their diseases. Piet Dieselmann, a transport rider, has overstated the merits of the hospital because he wants to boast about Platkops dorp. But Juriaan, the simple religious man, is filled with hope. He lifts his beloved wife onto his ox-wagon, settling her comfortably on the feather-bed which they have used for so many years, and they set off together for the hospital.

On their leisurely way, when Juriaan outspanned the oxen, "their hearts were filled with a quiet content."[1] Their faith, their life close to nature and their mutual love had given them a knowledge of harmony and a quiet joy. The simplicity of the old couple is at once contrasted against the world of the hospital. The resident doctor is a good man, but he cannot tell Juriaan or Deltje the full story of Deltje's pain. They are too uneducated to understand. The old woman must remain in the hospital, and he will do what he can to alleviate it. Deltje and Juriaan must part, and this separation breeds a pain in both their hearts which is far worse than the physical affliction.

Between Nurse Robert, the brisk, young, humanitarian woman in the hospital, and the spiritual, naïve van Royens there can be no contact. She thinks she knows what is best for them, refusing to believe Deltje when the old woman maintains that her pain has gone. The type of kindness which she and the hospital can offer "reached them only as the kindness of human beings reaches the suffering of dumb animals."[2] Nurse Robert is contemptuous of the Aangenaam Valley which the van Royens love. To her it is backward.

Pauline Smith reinforces the differences between the aged couple and the life of the hospital by contrasting descriptions. The van Royens' house is built from simple things, it stands close by the peach trees and the stream, merging with its surroundings. On the contrary, the hospital is one of the few new, stone buildings in Platkops dorp. It has not yet blended with the landscape. No trees or garden grow around it. Naked, unfruitful, square, it possesses none of the lines of nature. Even the water in van Royen's mountain home is different from that of the hospital. As Deltje lies alone in her narrow bed, she dreams of the brown and bubbling stream next to their cottage. She cannot drink the water from the hospital rain-tank easily, and Nurse Robert, who prefers this water to that from mountain streams, considers that she is making an unreasonable fuss.

At last, one quiet night, Juriaan steals into the hospital to fetch Deltje, and the couple trek away into the mountains. Deltje's pain has not been cured. She is dying. Yet her heart is filled once more with serenity. They are united again; Juriaan feels that his God has returned to him. The spiritual pain has proved worse than that of the body.

"The Pain" is a sad story. The reader is led to wonder what Juriaan will do when his beloved inevitably dies. And he too must die soon. It is frustrating that a couple so loving and wise should be so ignorant and vulnerable to inferior, if more sophisticated people. But there is also joy in the narrative. Some of the absolute contentment and faith of the van Royens is conveyed to the reader. He hears the tender words with which Juriaan speaks to his wife. He is moved by the patient way they wait outside the hospital until one of the staff deigns to notice them.

Finally, he is left in that mood of mourning and wonder which seems to rise in the human heart when it realises that love and all valuable qualities of character and mind must on the face of it inevitably be annihilated. This is the feeling evoked by tragedy, and insofar as "The Pain" creates this feeling it can be regarded as a tragic story.

II *"The Schoolmaster"*

In this story, young and innocent Engela comes to love Jan Boetje, a stranger who has turned up on the farm Nooitgedacht from nowhere. For six months he stays with the Delports and their grandchildren, teaching them to read and write and telling them about the distant parts of the world. Engela's love for him grows steadily. On a bright day in the middle of winter the girl drives out on an expedition with Jan Boetje and the young children. When the mules refuse to obey the schoolmaster at a nearby drift, a mood af madness seizes him. He slashes the animals across the eyes with his whip, then drags out a knife and blinds them. They rush away in panic with Jan Boetje running after them like a maniac. Engela is heartbroken. She comes to experience the grief and pain which love can bring.

After his fit of insanity has passed over, Jan Boetje is compelled by his conscience to pull a handcart through the empty veld, collecting things and selling them to eke out a living. Engela sends him her Bible via the toll-gate man. All through the summer she thinks of him, wondering how he is faring. At last when winter comes round again she has a feeling that he has attained peace.

> When I looked up through the open half-door, and saw, far above the orange grove, the peaks of the Zwartkops Mountains so pure and white against the blue sky, there came a strange sad happiness about my heart, and it was if if I knew that Jan Boetje had at last found peace and were on his way to tell me so.[3]

Jan Boetje does come to her—dead—drowned in the very drift where his madness had seized him. When his body is laid out at the farm, Engela goes to him, pressing her head against his breast. She is blinded by tears, yet ecstatic with an almost mystical joy. Through her heart run the words which her grandmother had spoken to her when she had first learned the bitterness of love: "My joy and my sorrow. . . . The light of my heart, and my treasure."[4]

The character of the strange, intense Jan Boetje is powerfully portrayed. He is the stranger, the man with a secret sin, coming from no fixed place, going to no certain destination. When he arrives he is "asking for shelter out of the storm."[5] There is something Mephistophelean about his little pointed beard and dark features. His pale hands and complexion are suggestive of death. To Engela he is like the Widow of Nain's son risen from the dead whom she had read about in grandmother Delport's Bible. In another place the reader is told explicitly that he arrived "as if from the dead."[6] At once he is appointed schoolmaster, teaching these innocent children about a larger world. Engela, a simple girl, has her eyes opened to places far beyond her own experience. And in return for the love which he has fostered in her she prays for him and teaches him about the plants in the veld.

After Jan Boetje has gone mad and run away, grandmother Delport asks Engela to take over the teaching. This she can do now, because through her love for the schoolmaster she has gained a wider experience. That strength can be gained through acceptance of harsh blows and disappointments is one of the ideas running through this story. Engela is ill and sensitive. Her love never reaches fulfilment, and she can come to know only resignation and a mystical serenity. Her hopeless affection is contrasted sadly against the rich fullness of Mevrouw Delport. The young woman says of her:

> I had seen once a ship come sailing into Zandtbaai harbour, and grandmother walking, in her full, wide skirts with Aunt Betje's children bobbing like little boats around her, would make me often think of it.[7]

But even this "big, wise and gentle woman"[8] who has had so satisfying a life realises that "love comes at the last to be but what one makes it."[9]

Although the action of Pauline Smith's short stories often develops at a leisurely pace, keeping time with her slow, serious characters and the unchanging landscape, she can present an incident occupying but a few seconds with dramatic effect. Such an incident occurs at the Rooikrantz drift. Engela, Jan Boetje, and the children have been driving for fifteen minutes when they come to the river. The banks are steep and on the far side are the red rocks which give the place its name.

> Here the wild bees make their honey, and the white wild geese have their home. And that day how beautiful in the still clear air were the great red rocks against the blue sky, and how beautiful against the rocks were the white wings of the wild geese.[10]

Here again, in new words, is the vivid child's description of the drift in *Platkops Children*. Engela feels about the scene as a child might, responding to it with a naïve spontaneity. She is without guile. For her the rocks, the geese, the sky, and the water form a harmonious whole. Nature is in a state of intense animation.

The grandchildren go down to the river's edge, and Engela and the schoolmaster are left alone in the cart. There has been something exciting about this journey, a thrill and lilt of the blood, as if some revelation is to be made, an intimacy to be shown. This is the ripe time. Then the mules begin to disobey. They will not move when Jan Boetje whips them up. Why does he whip them up? The reader is not told. Pauline Smith handles the onset of the schoolmaster's madness outstandingly. It springs quite credibly from the moment of heightened emotion, and we do not perceive where his sanity leaves off and his madness begins.

He strikes at the mules. Then when they will not move, he jumps down and slashes them over the eyes. Each blow of his whip cuts not only into the sensitive eyeballs of the animals, but also into Engela's innocence and the trust which she has extended to him. Before the young woman knows where she is, Jan Boetje has changed completely. "His face that had grown so dear to me, was terrible to see."[11] In a flash all her confidence is shattered. She learns that people are unpredictable and that things are not always what they seem.

As Engela tries to climb down from the cart, Jan Boetje plunges his knife into the eyes of the mules. So sudden is this development that the reader thrills with terror. Yet this lunatic cruelty is made believable by what has gone before. Engela falls to the ground and the mules go rushing down the stream bed. The change has been so quick it is almost unreal to her. She looks down to the drift where the children still clap their hands and the geese still fly amongst the rocks. Thus it seems that her old world exists for a fraction of a second after it has been destroyed.

Pauline Smith's first aim is to chronicle the key events and experiences in the lives of her characters, and it does not concern her whether they take years or seconds to play themselves out. Engela, Jan Boetje, and the grandchildren probably change as much in the split second as they did in the whole six months preceding.

The schoolmaster, the cart, and the mules are far down the stream. The scene is one of cacophony and chaos. The cart, which should ride smoothly, is bumping; the wood is splintering; the man who should be leading the mules and driving the cart is on foot and in pursuit of the mules. The mules who should see are blind, and their persecutor who should have the light of reason is once more in darkness. The sin and sorrow of which he spoke to grandmother Delport has asserted itself again, despite the simple farm life which could have taught him peace, and in the face of the love shown him by the young woman.

III *"The Miller"*

Andries Lombard, the miller, is "a stupid kindly man whom illness has turned into a morose and bitter one."[12] When life had been going well for him, he felt at rest in his community, got on well with his wife and children, and believed that he was loved by God. Now that he was sick he thought that God was making him suffer, and he, in his turn, determined to make his wife suffer. There are no middle shades in the miller's view of life. Either all is well, or all is ill—black or white. He tells his wife, Mintje, that when he is dead Meneer van der Merwe will drive her and their children from the house and the land, although he knows very well that the farmer is a generous and just man. It is from pigheadedness that he chooses to see things this way.

The farm community of Harmonie to which the mill is attached is peaceful and stable. Pauline Smith wants to convey the strong faith she sensed in the country people of the Little Karoo and the joy which appeared to exist in a social order of this kind. The symbolism in the names is transparently clear. Harmonie, Meneer van de Merwe's farm, is the Afrikaans for harmony. It is situated in the Aangenaam, or pleasant, valley near the Aangenaam River. Close by the farmhouse stands a square, white-washed church which has been raised by Meneer van der Merwe for the people of the valley. The farmer is a Godfearing, patient man; the neat, restrained, and orderly building is an outward sign of his inner virtues. Around the church are four white paths made from the stone which the farmer's sons had dug out of the mountains in a fruitless search for gold. Meneer van der Merwe had been overjoyed and had quoted from the Bible: "It is well, my children! The judgments of the Lord are more to be desired than gold, yea, than much fine gold."[13]

It is against this forthright, untainted community that Andries Lombard sets his face. He places himself in opposition to its life and routine. When, in the spring, the other men begin to plant their lands, he will not follow suit. No man will have the benefit of his crops when he is dead, he says. Mintje, his faithful wife, whom he had once loved dearly, calling her his dove, has become a frightened hen, characterless, ruled by power only. As the months go by, his rebellious, tyrannous fits grow worse. He is moving in the opposite direction to the ripening year, and is further estranged from love. At this time, however, a remnant of the affection he had for Mintje still lingers in his memory.

There were days when Andries, having driven Mintje away from him, would have given all the world to call her back again to speak with her of his sorrow and his love.[14]

Finally, in autumn, as the crops are being gathered in, he digs a grave for himself in his naked lands. This grave is sterile, a painful thing to see. It is in utter contradiction to the time of harvest-home and thanksgiving. Mintje is reduced to tears. But he has done this to make her suffer. When she asks him if he will come to the thanksgiving service at the Harmonie Church, he asks her sardonically if it is for his grave that she wants to go and thank God.

The miller's wife is driven away, and the children follow her down to the thanksgiving service. As his family moves away from him, the children calling to one another amongst the rocks, a mood of desolation sweeps across Andries Lombard. He wishes that his wife will turn and call to him. Then he will go to her. But his moods of the past months have forced him willy-nilly into isolation. Mintje is too scared to look back.

Sitting by himself, the miller begins to feel dizzy and ill. He thinks of the Jew-woman who runs the shop in Harmonie. When she first appeared at a Thanksgiving she had been old, bent and thin, cringing like a hunted animal. She had suffered terrible things in Europe before she escaped. Yet she had not become embittered. Her gift to her first harvest festival had been a cake. This act of generosity had been returned in the same spirit by the community. Mevrouw van der Merwe herself had answered, "Is not your Lord also my Lord?"[15] and had taken the cake to the thank-offering table. As he thinks of the Jew-woman, the miller remembers his wife:

. . . if it was the terrible things that had happened to her in her own country that had turned the Jew-woman into a frightened animal, it was he, Andries, who had turned Mintje into a nervous hen.[16]

Suddenly he realises that his proud anger has got him nowhere.

He is cut off from the community and from his family. Moreover, he has victimised his wife. Ill, his head swimming, he starts walking down towards the church. He feels he cannot go to the Thanksgiving because he has nothing to bring. God is withdrawn; but he will go back to his wife.

From the homestead the miller goes into the grove of poplars next to the church. These trees, with their golden leaves, are beautiful and delicate, the handiwork of a more gentle God than He who had been Andries Lombard's overlord in the past few months. The miller is seriously ill now, his ears humming, a pressure in his throat. In a single moment of clarity he hears the Pastor say that a broken and contrite heart can be as pleasing to God as gifts. Ironically, the assembled congregation, whom he has been rejecting, does not notice him. It is the Jew-woman, who always stood apart from the service, who comes to his aid.

Andries Lombard is dying. Pauline Smith is no weaver of facile tales nor a creator of cut-and-dried symbolism. The miller cannot speak, and the Jew-woman leads him *away* from the service to her store. But he must be reconciled with Mintje. By so doing he will atone for his attitude to God and man through the months of his illness. In his agony to explain to her, he tears the eelskin talisman, which Mintje had fetched for him, from his throat.

He stumbled, and as he stumbled blood rushed from his mouth soaking his beard, his shirt, his coat sleeves.[17]

At last the Jew-woman understands. She runs to fetch Mintje. When Andries Lombard is at last reconciled to his wife and God he is on the point of death. He can speak no words to ask forgiveness. There is no happy life after reconciliation. Only the "vague, weak movement"[18] of his arm; and the miller falls dead onto the leaves.

IV *"The Sinner"*

Niklaas Dampers is a *bywoner* working for a hard, embittered farmer, Meneer van Reenen. He has always thought of himself as righteous. Fearing the Lord, he was confident that at the end

God would deal justly with him and chastise the other terrible sinners in the Platkops district. He prays to God that his favourite daughter may remain with him always, but she marries and moves to the Philip district. God has not answered him and he is filled with resentment and fear. Toontje, his silent wife, is as inscrutable as the Lord, angering him almost to insanity. He flees from her, going for relief to the arms of Jacoba Nooi.

The intention of this story is to show how Niklaas comes to learn resignation and to realise that he is in no position to judge others. Pauline Smith explores the effects of self-righteousness and acceptance in a number of ways.

Jacoba Nooi, the woman to whom the *bywoner* goes, is plump, trivial, and talkative. She is unmarried and, unlike the other women of her age, dresses in a fancy cotton gown and a hat trimmed with ribbons. Jacoba's role as a temptress is soon made clear. Her name, Nooi, is Afrikaans for young lady or sweetheart, and, as a verb, means to invite. One of her prize possessions is a little mirror ringed with shells, which she uses in such a way as to cause comment amongst the other women. Niklaas Dampers has not heard the whispers about Jacoba. He has been too introspective, wrapped up in his own ideas about God and his wife. Consequently, she is able to lure him down to the river bank and gradually to make him desire her. The reader is expected to notice particularly the way in which she uses her mirror to fascinate him.

The *bywoner* has not been accustomed to seeing the image of his face. Jacoba twists the mirror round to show him his image again and again. Finally he becomes drunk with the experience, forgetting the world around him and his self-control. This same mirror is in the hands of Jacoba Nooi some time later when she is flirting with the *bywoner's* new young master. She kept it in "a little card-board box shaped like a coffin."[19] It represents an unreal world which can lead only to emptiness and delusion. Niklaas Dampers does not know this yet. As he sees it, there is no justice, sin, or need for conscience in life. He abandons both his family and everything he stood for to live with Jacoba Nooi in the Kombuis, a district to the North of Meneer van Reenen's farm.

When the old, hard farmer had been a young man, he and

Toontje, Niklaas Dampers's wife, had been lovers in that very place. She had been "free and beautiful to him as a roe-buck in the mountains."[20] Toontje visits Meneer van Reenen and tells him that Niklaas has abandoned her to live with Jacoba Nooi and work the tobacco lands of a young, ambitious Hollander. If there is anything that can enrage the testy, dying farmer, it is the word tobacco. Growing this crop was his only remaining interest. He lashes out in anger and self-righteousness against the *bywoner*: "May his soul burn in hell and Koba's also."[21]

Gently, Toontje reminds him of their past. They too have loved one another madly, sinfully in the Kombuis: "is it for Mijnheer and me to judge him?"[22] she asks. Here Pauline Smith carries further her exploration of self-righteousness. Although a man may be forgiven for his past errors, the fact that he has committed them strips him of the right to judge anyone else for the same fault. Toontje brings the old farmer to realise this, and he agrees to say that he has sent Niklaas to work for the Hollander.

In the Kombuis the *bywoner's* conscience begins to assert itself once more. Although Jacoba Nooi is talkative, he finds that she is just as secretive, if not more, than Toontje. Toontje's silence, like that of his God, had infuriated him because he was trying to know what was unknowable. He had not understood that there were beings outside of him, whose life and thoughts eluded his black-and-white conceptions of the world. With Jacoba, on the other hand, he could never be sure. She was always running round him with her words.

Niklaas Dampers begins to change. His belief in God and his fear of sin return. But now "he who had once counted himself among the elect now knew himself to be among the damned."[23] He sees a great gulf fixed between good and evil, but no longer has the pride to consider himself one of the angels. Gradually he comes to suspect that his mistress is transferring her affections from him to the young Hollander. He finds her near the farmer's house, flashing her mirror in the sun. When he questions her, she is half-threatening, half-elusive, leaving him bewildered. Like the looking-glass, she is not satisfying, merely reflecting back his own anxious state of mind.

Finally, when he comes early one day from the fields, tormented and miserable, he finds her sitting close to the Hollander, giggling and luring the man on with the inevitable little mirror. This identical seduction-play hurts Niklaas deeply. In a flash he realises that Jacoba's promises and Jacoba's delights, which he had sinned so much to have, mean absolutely nothing. He goes home, takes up his possessions and the bundle of clothes which Toontje had sent him a long time before, and sets out. Now he does not even have the dubious pride of being a grand sinner. He is just a hopeless fool. For the first time in his life he does not know where he is going.

In this state he arrives at the crossroads. One way is to Philip dorp and his daughter Saartje. A second is to Platkops where, as far as he knows, his wife and children have been turned out by Meneer van Reenen. The third is to the Malgas district, a waterless desert, and a fitting home for an outcast. This is a true crossroads of choice in the life of Niklaas Dampers. He decides that he must go towards Malgas, because he has no right to make demands either on his wife or his daughter now. Weak, suffering, and repentant, he turns in to a prickly-pear thicket to sit down and rest.

He is swept by a mood of utter desolation. The man who at one time considered himself a righteous soul, who thought that he knew the workings of God's mind, is now empty and humble. He turns his eyes to a cluster of red flowers; they remind him of the burning bush where the Lord spoke to Moses. "But the Lord never now spoke to His people, and who was he, a sinner from the Kombuis, that the Lord should speak to him?"[24]

Niklaas Dampers, who knew and expected everything, now expects nothing. As he arranges his bundles to push on to Malgas, the note which Toontje had written so long ago flutters to the ground. In this she tells Niklaas how Meneer van Reenen has allowed her to remain in their house and of the story the farmer told about his *bywoner's* disappearance to the Kombuis. Her own experience in the Kombuis is summed up in the sentence she adds to the letter; "God forgive me, Niklaas, if I should judge you, for there is not one of us that has not sinned."[25]

Gratefully, the *bywoner* accepts her forgiveness. God has spoken in pity, an attribute of His which Niklaas has come to know only through misery. He does not concern himself with thoughts of damnation or salvation any longer, for who can judge those things but God? Instead he accepts the Lord's kindness with tears and repentance, and sets off for Platkops dorp to be reconciled with his wife as soon as possible.

V *"Anna's Marriage"*

This story is told by Griet, the elder daughter in a family of seven children. Anna, the youngest, was favoured by the mother, and when Griet chose her own husband, the mother determined that she would provide a better match for the younger girl. She persuaded her husband to buy the farm Brandtwacht as a dowry for Anna, because she had always imagined that Blaukops, a farm which was given with Griet, would have been assigned to her favourite. Moreover, she got her husband to build a fine house for Anna at Brandtwacht.

On account of all this, there was friction between Griet and her mother. When Philip Coetzee, a shiftless, weak man, came down to the Platkops district to look for gold, he was able to exploit this antagonism. Blaukops and Brandtwacht stood on adjacent land, and Philip bribed an old man, Jan Jafta, to lie to Griet's mother that her husband, Otto, was leading Brandt-wacht's water onto his own farm. Otto and Ludovic, one of Griet's brothers, wanted to reason with their mother, but Griet would not allow them to go. Self-righteous and angry, she condemns her mother and will have nothing more to do with her. Even when she hears that her mother is suffering with lameness, she will not see her.

This open rift between mother and daughter is just what Philip Coetzee wants. He goes to the mother's farm, Welgevonden, waits, pretending to look for gold, and makes love to Anna. When Jan Jafta sees himself how the girl has fallen in love with Philip he goes to the mother and confesses how he has lied. When Griet hears this, she realises that she has been partly responsible for this outcome. She rushes at once to her mother and they are reconciled. But it is too late to save Anna. Griet goes to her sister's room and remonstrates with her. She tells her how Philip Coetzee deserted Johanna Marincowitz after he had made her father bankrupt. She takes Anna in her arms and shakes her, but she is powerless against the young girl's love for Philip Coetzee.

Because of her selfish love, Anna's mother has withheld experience from her, not really allowing her to grow up. Griet's wounded pride has made her blind to the fact that the rift between her and mother would let Philip Coetzee gain Anna's affection. They paid little attention to Anna when they were able. Now that their own weaknesses have given the lying man the whiphand and their eyes are opened to Anna's predicament, it is too late to help her.

Anna and Philip Coetzee marry. He buys her expensive furniture, and when he sees that this delights her, continues to get more and more. As the young woman sinks slowly into an unreal world, her family is shocked into an appreciation of hard fact. Once her mother had thought that no suitor in all the Platkops district was good or rich enough for her Anna. Her selfish dreaming is over now, and she wonders anxiously with Griet how Philip Coetzee can afford to buy the red plush sofa he has brought to Anna's house. Inevitably Philip Coetzee falls into debt and bonds some of the Brandtwacht lands in payment. He brings home a black musical box which plays three tunes when you turn the handle. Anna is fascinated and when her brother Ludovic comes round to talk about the bond, she refuses to listen to him. "Listen now, brother, to the music that comes from this little black box that Philip has given me!"[26] she says twice. The repetition of these words is eerie in effect. Anna is mad with love for Philip Coetzee, and all can see it.

At last, when Brandtwacht has to be sold to cover Philip Coetzee's debts, the young woman's trusting and simple nature is contrasted against the sordid reality in a sad, ironical scene. A Jew is sent round to make a list of the furniture which is to be sold to pay Philip's debts. Philip tells her that the man is a friend, and she must show him round the house. "Anna was proud as a child to do this."[27]

Right to the end Anna is the victim of other people's shortcomings and of circumstance. When Ludovic learns by chance that the farm is to be sold up, he rides to Thys, Rijk, and Andries and sends for Lombard. Each of the brothers rides to Brandtwacht and then off to the store where the farm is to be sold.

Only when the last of them, Lombard, arrives does Anna learn what is happening. The brothers buy back the farm between them and plan to settle it on Anna for life. But they are so concerned about the family's honour that none of them thinks she might be alone and that Philip Coetzee will almost certainly have deserted her. For that day and the whole of the night, Anna is left alone in the house at Brandtwacht with the shock of Lombard's terrible news. Only when Griet realises what has happened does she rush to the farm.

She sat on the red plush sofa and already her cheeks were flushed with the fever that was soon to kill her. On her lap she held the little black box that Philip had given her, but though she turned the handle there came no sound from it.[28]

The reader is shocked by this ending. Anna's disappointment has been so great that her mind has been unable to take it. She is ill and almost mad. Yet the conclusion follows on naturally from what has gone before. Pauline Smith has kept him so busy following the brothers in their bid to buy back the farm that he too has had little time to think of Anna's solitary hours.

No tunes come from Anna's music box. It is as unreal as the life which Philip Coetzee offered her. Yet this story seems to say that she is not alone in her pathetic, false position. Griet and her mother have both shown themselves to be unrealistic before her, the mother in thinking that there was no suitor marvellous enough for Anna, and Griet in refusing to acknowledge her responsibilities to her mother. All three women have shown pig-headed determination and their stubborness has led all of them into false positions.

VI *"The Pastor's Daughter"*

Niccoline Johanna, the pastor's daughter, is the kind of person Pauline Smith admires. She is drawn in a sombre, serious light. First her family, and later circumstances, seem to be against her ever marrying Paul Marais. When she meets Paul for the first time, he is brought to her father's house in Platkops dorp by Jan Cloete, a neighbouring farmer. At that stage she is zestful and childlike. She remembers how Jan Cloete's beard wagged and was impressed by the forceful manner in which Paul talked about his English grandmother. They fall head-over-heels in love. Niccoline Johanna confesses:

It was as if it must kill me if I could not be alone with Paul. Yes, love is like that—beautiful and cruel and selfish and bitter, and who can tell where one begins and the other ends!²⁹

Now Niccoline Johanna is called upon to make her first bitter act of self-denial. One day in the linen room she tells her mother that she is going to marry Paul Marais. What follows is one of the most dramatic and realistic scenes in Pauline Smith's writing. Her mother pleads with her to stay. Niccoline backs against the wall, saying that she *will* go with Paul. Then "breathing hard like a horse"³⁰ her mother begins to unbutton her bodice. Niccoline is terrified, thinking she has gone mad. Then the daughter sees the cancer of the breast which is soon to kill the older woman. Her mother asks her to stay, because her father is a simple, impractical man, and there will be no one to look after him when she dies. In this passage the reader can appreciate the lifelike and moving way in which the conflict between mother and daughter is shown. Pauline Smith never shrinks from unpleasant or frightening facts.

Niccoline Johanna turns Paul Marais down. He is very upset and feels that she has broken her promise. Her mother makes it more difficult for her by speaking afterwards of Paul's good points: "it was as if God had taken me up into a high mountain like Moses and was showing me the things that would never be mine,"³¹ Niccoline says. Heroically, she tells the white lie that she will go to Paul later, so that her mother will not worry.

Now, in a bitter stroke of fate, Niccoline's father dies before her mother. The very reason for which she turned down Paul Marais is proved to have been vain. Blow follows blow. On the day of her father's funeral she hears that Paul Marais has married an Englishwoman in the Transvaal. Instead of going to pieces, Niccoline lives quietly in a small house given to her by the Church Council. For ten years she earns a living by selling home-grown vegetables at the market. Then she hears that

Paul Marais's wife has run away. Another three years, and late one night Paul Marais appears on the step of her house. Paul has come to ask her forgiveness, admitting that he has misunderstood her in the past. She has broken no promises and he has to confess that his idea that all Englishwomen are marvellous is a wrong one. He hears that his wife is dead and asks Niccoline to marry him. "So surely as I live I will do it!"[32] she replies. There are no reservations in her words. She has not grown timid or neurotic in the intervening time.

Paul has to go away and settle up some land; then he will return and they will marry. It appears that Niccoline is to see her love for him fulfilled at last. But again circumstances cross her cruelly and, it seems, unnecessarily. One night Paul returns, exhausted, to say that he has come across his wife in a toll-house in the Philip district. She has implored him to take her back. What must he do? he asks Niccoline.

Through her experiences and self-denial the heroine of the story has gained in strength, whereas Paul, for the moment, is demoralised. She has now outstripped him in determination and in power of decision. Without hesitation she advises him to go back to his wife. All her happiness shattered again, Niccoline weeps bitterly. For some time after she is so depressed that she thinks she will not be able to live. Later she hears that Paul's wife is expecting a baby. The couple wish to name it after her, but she asks them to call it by her mother's name. Paul is far gone in consumption when his wife dies.

At last there is no barrier between Niccoline and her lover. But now he is a hopeless invalid. She leaves at once for the Transvaal to nurse him. He proves querulous and difficult. She has the additional rebuff of being rejected by Paul in his last days. The last week of his life he lies with his face to the wall and will speak to no one. He dies speaking of his grandmother the Englishwoman.

Niccoline Johanna returns to Platkops dorp with Paul Marais's child, Christoffeline. She is not soured by her experiences: "on her strong sallow face there was neither bitterness nor sorrow, only a quiet resignation."[33] She has gained a serenity of mind tempered by sadness and a quiet content. Life is on her side. She is caring for Paul's daughter. Christoffeline is named after her mother, who had made marriage with Paul impossible. The wedding dress she was sewing when Paul arrived to say that he could not marry her, is now being turned into a dress for the girl. Niccoline is still living in her slow, austere way long after all the other persons who are caught up in the unhappy events are dead.

VII "Ludovitje"

This is a brief, emotionally charged story of a little boy who had religious intuitions which seemed to border on the mystical. Just before his death, he converts an African worker on his father's farm to Christianity. Emerging from the description and the action is a brooding, yet sweet sadness. From the beginning, people outside Ludovitje's family think that he is weak in the head. His mother, Alida, defends him immediately. She feels that he has an understanding of the ways of God, and that the joy of God is in his heart. One of the purposes of the story is to show that Ludovitje's life does have an effect on the world of everyday action.

The boy's grandfather has just died when a band of Africans come from the Tali district to dig a dam in the mountains for his father. On the one hand, there is the sensitive boy, grieving for the dead man and yearning for death and what is beyond; on the other, there are the Africans, engaging in solid, everyday work. But Ludovitje is able to move them. When he comes to the dam with his father, singing his psalm, these Africans, who are completely heathen, stop in their work to listen to him. His world lures them, giving them a strange sense of harmony and joy. The words which Pauline Smith gives the boy are significant: "Tremble, thou earth, at the presence of the Lord, at the presence of the God of Jacob, Who turned the hard rock into a standing water and the flintstone into a springing well."[34] Some parallel is implied between the work of the Africans and Ludovitje's "work" in trying to get people to understand his God.

As the digging of the dam progresses, the reader realises that Ludovitje is working in the hearts of his father and mother and especially in that of "Maqwasi the Kaffir."[35] If Maqwasi is the strongest of the diggers, making it possible for the desolate Credo

Valley to become a great dam, he is also the one in whose stony heart a miracle is achieved through the influence of the boy. Ludovitje is also doing his "digging" to change the rock into a standing water.

The boy's death forms the climax of the story. Maqwasi asks permission to leave his work and go down to the farmhouse, where he is converted. The African and the scholars from the local school are drawn together in a single bond of mingled sadness and joy as they sing the 114th Psalm at Ludovitje's request.

After the boy's death, Maqwasi comes to his father and asks permission to dig a grave for him in the *koppie* which faces the mountains. This strikes the African as an appropriate place, no doubt because the feeling of closeness to God that he gets in the mountains is similar to the feeling he had when he was in company with Ludovitje. Piet asks Maqwasi how he will succeed in digging the iron-hard clay-stone. Maqwasi replies, with simple dignity, that he has dug a dam in the mountains and can he not now dig a grave? Again we see the impact which Ludovitje had upon the Africans and the world of everyday labour which they represent. Maqwasi is so thankful for his conversion that he is now prepared to devote his energy to the hard job of digging a grave in clay-stone for the child. Ludovitje's life has also helped to develop love and understanding between the farmer and his African labourers. Piet invites Maqwasi to stay on at the farm and, for the sake of the child, offers to treat him well.

This story shows the marked influence of Biblical style on Pauline Smith's writing, e.g., the concluding paragraph:

So Maqwasi dug for us graves in the clay-stone. One on each side of the child he dug them, and left us, and went again to his own people, spreading the Word of God among them.[36]

This sentence could, as far as rhythm and phraseology are concerned, have come directly from the New Testament. In "Why and How I became an Author" she records her discovery that the conversational rhythms of the Little Karoo people could be reproduced successfully in a type of Biblical English.[37] Here she uses her Biblical model most successfully. It is something which goes beyond dialogue; which has discerned a real parallel between the lives of the *bywoners* of the Little Karoo and those of the characters in the Bible stories. The Biblical atmosphere is in no way forced upon the story, and the effect is moving and natural.

VIII   *"The Sisters"*

This story has as its theme one of the questions which seem to have seized hold of Pauline Smith's imagination with an especial force. Ought one to judge or to forgive? What is the aftermath of sin?

Burgert de Jager is the owner of the farm Zeekoegatt. Although he knew that Jan Redlinghuis, a neighbouring farmer, had his water-rights fixed by law, he persisted in fighting for the right to lead a furrow from the Ghamka River, until he had no money left. Jan Redlinghuis's farm is called Bitterwater, and by involving himself with it Burgert has indeed embittered his life and that of his family. He has judged what he thought was good for his wife: she must have a fine dress and live in a house in Platkops dorp, when all she wanted was peace in the house. In bitterness and sadness of heart she died. Finally, in an act of madness, Burgert bonds some of his own farm to Jan Redlinghuis. Now his opponent is in a position to turn him into a poor White. But Redlinghuis offers to marry his daughter, Marta, instead.

Burgert now has to choose between his daughter and his farm. He knows well that Jan Redlinghuis is an evil man, given to strange fits of madness, but he still prefers to sacrifice Marta and gain the furrow of water from the Ghamka River. Marta is loving and submissive. She knows that life will be difficult with Jan Redlinghuis, but she tries to think the best of him. Burgert's second daugther, Sukey, is of a more determined spirit. She foresees that marrying Jan Redlinghuis will ruin Marta, and she is indignant at her father's behaviour. Judging both men bitterly in her heart she goes and offers herself to Jan Redlinghuis in Marta's place. He refuses her.

Wrangling over the water-rights has also affected Jan Redlinghuis, who has acted cruelly and spitefully towards the de Jagers during the whole affair. Now his sense of guilt and his bitterness turn him crazy, and he takes the submissive Marta around in a cart, crying out to all and sundry to look at the wife whom Burgert de Jager sold to him. The reader realises that this is as much an indictment of Redlinghuis, who bought the wife, as of the man who sold her.

At Zeekoegatt, Sukey insists that Burgert face what he has done. When he tries to escape from his conscience and reality by saying that Marta has a fine tent-cart in which to drive, she replies that Marta is driving to her grave. For her, the water which Burgert is leading onto the land is like blood. Her mother died and her sister was sold for it. Sukey has vowed that if Marta is allowed to marry Jan Redlinghuis, she will know that there is no God. Entrenched in her righteousness, she judges both God and her father. The "blood" which Burgert is running onto his fields symbolises the continuance of her father's sin.

Jan Redlinghuis's sense of guilt grows stronger and stronger. He realises that his old idea of an eye for an eye and a tooth for a tooth has led only to sorrow and emptiness of heart. When Marta is dying and Sukey comes over to nurse her, he asks her a disturbing and eccentric question.

"See here, Sukey de Jager! Which of us now had the greatest sin—your father who sold me his daughter Marta, or I who bought her? Marta who let herself be sold, or you who offered yourself to save her?"[38]

For him it is a vicious circle from which he cannot escape. As his wife lies dying, he wanders off into the mountains and dies of exhaustion. Marta dies, and at last her father sees that he cannot run the Ghamka water onto his land any longer. He admits that it is "blood" in that furrow, and he asks God to forgive him for what he has done. Sukey sees more clearly than he that, though a man may be forgiven for what he has done, the consequences can never be wiped out completely.

It was in my heart to say to him: "The blood is already so deep in the lands that nothing we can do will now wash it out."[39]

Pauline Smith presents Sukey's conception in a vivid way. A man may no longer be aware of his sin (blood sunk deep into the land), yet its results are diffused throughout his life. We can see clearly the different implications of blood in the land and blood running in the furrow. In the former it can be controlled no longer; in the latter it can be stopped at will. The blood in the furrow suggests persistence in the same sin. The blood in the land is the aftermath of sin which has been repented. It may even cause new foliage to grow on the land. Through repentance a man may become better, but it is only because of his past sin that he can achieve the new state. Sukey realises all this, and yet she says nothing to her father. She has learned that she is not in a position to judge others.

CHAPTER 6

The Beadle

ARNOLD BENNETT provided the introduction to the first edition of *The Little Karoo* when it was published in 1925. He wrote there that when people asked him who Pauline Smith was, he would reply, "She is a novelist."[1] Though she had completed no novels at that time, he was confident that she had it in her to do so.

The eight stories of the 1925 edition all seem to contribute in some way to a single imaginative district. Almost all of them mention Platkops dorp. Far out from the village lie the Aangenaam Valley and the community of Harmonie which are the background for "The Pain" and "The Miller." Farms nearer in are the settings for "The Schoolmaster," "The Sinner," "Anna's Marriage," "Ludovitje," and "The Sisters." "The Pastor's Daughter" is set in Platkops dorp itself. It must have been clear to Arnold Bennett that Pauline Smith's preoccupation with this large area and great variety of characters might possibly lead to an idea which could not be contained easily within the bounds of a short story. And so he encouraged her to produce the novel which he felt the scope of her vision demanded.

For the setting of *The Beadle* she chose the outlying area of the Aangenaam Valley and the isolated community of Harmonie. Meneer van der Merwe, the slow, patient farmer from "The Miller," appears again with his wife. The miller himself has become a subsidiary character. The Jew-woman and her nephew also appear.

From the start a patriarchal and conservative society is described. Most of its members have slow, definite ways, simple speech, and strong faith. Pauline Smith's method of characterisation reinforces the impression of a community where every man has his place. Her men and women are clearly and briefly described, physical and temperamental characteristics alike.

Aalst Vlokman, the beadle, "was a short, strong-willed, friendless man with small brown eyes and a small, reddish beard."[2] Body and temperament are akin to each other. The reddish beard tells us of the beadle's passion and the small eyes of his narrow, dogmatic ways. Similarly, Mevrouw van der Merwe:

She was a big, gentle woman, capable and kind. All children and young people loved her and found comfort for the troubles of their age in her serenity and tenderness, in her low, clear voice and in her smile which, in lighting up her own rather full and heavy face, seemed also to light up the hearts of those upon whom it fell.[3]

Mevrouw's physical characteristics and her good nature are inseparable. Her size is part and parcel of her kindliness. In order to stress her tenderness Pauline Smith points to her full and heavy face which lit up so often in a smile.

Though the characterisation is relatively static, ascribing a few definite and unchanging qualities to each person, the reader feels that he is in touch with what is real in them. The dialogue also is frequently concerned with showing only their essential characteristics. Altogether this makes for a lack of fluidity which, on some occasions, gives to the characters a monumental depth and grandeur, as for instance in this clash between Jan Beyers, an unsuccessful suitor to Andrina, and Aalst Vlokman.

The beadle was turning away from the trestle-table which he had put up in front of the church door for the thank-offerings of the women when Jan Beyers addressed him.

"Tell me now beadle," he said . . . "you that once offered me two plough-oxen for Andrina du Toit, that men thought was an orphan— is it true that she has gone now to her father, Herman du Toit, in the Losberg district?"

Strange as had been the young man's first question to him in spring, it had brought him no surprise. Now, for the first time since Jacoba's death, he was roused from his apathy to so intense and sudden an amazement and anxiety that he cried out as if in pain:

"Who says it?"

"No what, beadle," answered Jan Beyers, withdrawing slightly, married man though he was, from the bachelor Aalst Vlokman, "no what! Juffrouw de Neysen says it. Up in the post-office. To many of us there she has said it. Is it not then true, beadle?"

In a voice of such bitter contempt that it robbed the young man of whatever support his married state had hitherto afforded him, Aalst Vlokman answered.

"And what is it to you, Jan Beyers, whether or not Andrina du Toit has gone to her father in the Losberg district? Are you not now a married man with a sewing machine?"[4]

The clash between the two men is full-blooded and direct. There are no special graces, no conversational circumlocutions to hide or temper their real feelings. Aalst Vlokman is deeply involved, because this is his illegitimate daughter about whom Jan Beyers is speaking. Jan is an unsuccessful suitor to Andrina, and he too is moved in a basic human way. The slow, brooding lives of the characters and the limited powers of their conversation add to the impression one gets of an elemental conflict. Occasionally in this novel and in the short stories, one is reminded of the characters in ancient Greek plays, limited in movement by their stilts and closely clinging robes, robbed of many facial expressions by the conventional type masks which they wore, yet gaining through these limitations a greater power and presence, a larger-than-life identity.

Pauline Smith has another method of giving her characters a definite place in the community. She provides some of them with a physical environment in which they are at home and with which they have more connexions than any of the other people in the novel. Mevrouw van der Merwe has her kitchen in the Harmonie homestead, a large, genial place reflecting her character. Hans Rademeyer, the tender, compassionate wagon-driver who took in Andrina after she had been forced out of Antoinette's household in the Caroline district, has for his appropriate setting the wandering ox-wagon. To Andrina he is like Christ grown to be an old man: rootless, without possessions, all-accepting beneath the sky. He reaches serenity by relinquishing worldly concerns.

Tan' Linda de Neysen's post office closely reflects her character.

Its cluttered table and harness-bedraggled walls suggest her fussy muddleheadedness. We are told that the official postal service was not the natural means for passing on news in the outlying areas of the Little Karoo:

The Dutchman, living almost as close to nature as the native himself, learnt his news from the spoors on the veld and the roadside, from the passing of carts and wagons, from the flight of birds, from the trembling of a bush, from the sudden cry of an animal in distress breaking the silence of the mountain-side.[5]

The government post-cart and the postal regulations are intrusions from the greater world outside, which the country people do not wholly understand. Tan' Linda herself does not comprehend them completely. She leaves the book of postal regulations untouched, and the weights of the official weighing machine have long since been replaced by "a flat-iron, little bundles of pence and half pence tied up with string, two smooth flat stones and a hammer-head."[6]

Tan' Linda's understanding of the ways of the civilized world is as incomplete as her grasp of the postal system. In many ways she represents the dangers of partial knowledge. She is the one to think Harry will be a good husband for Andrina. With humorous ineptitude she tries to use the girl's ancestry as a bait to lure the Englishman. She arranges and secretly encourages what she believes to be a stunning match. In this way she makes it easier for Harry to seduce Andrina, but when Harry leaves after getting the girl pregnant, she condemns him roundly. "No what, Alida!" she says to Mevrouw van der Merwe. "The young man should have told us now when he came to us that there was one that waited for him in England."[7] The silly, romantic writer of love-letters for all the young men in the community cannot admit that she is partly to blame; she refuses to acknowledge that she has meddled with things beyond her depth. Alida van der Merwe, less sophisticated, yet wiser on account of her simplicity and love, is amazed that Tan' Linda could have thought seriously of Andrina for the Englishman.

"The Miller," "The Sinner," "Anna's Marriage," and "The Sisters" show Pauline Smith's interest in self-righteous and forgiving attitudes in men and women. As she sees it, self-righteousness leads a man to set too high a standard of perfection for himself and others. He judges them excessively, and this leads him to be dissatisfied with God. Love is frozen in him, and his friends desert him until he is left alone. On the other hand, a man who is resigned himself and does not judge others comes into closer contact with God and his neighbours. Aalst Vlokman, the beadle, from whom this book takes its title, is one of the hard, self-righteous men of whom, the Miller, the Sinner, and Meneer van Reenen are earlier examples.

At the outset of the novel, Vlokman is strong-willed and friendless. One of his chief characteristics is a bitterness of spirit. People are driven from him, and "in the long Aangenaam Valley there was no man who called him friend, no child who called him Oom."[8] The beadle has imposed himself upon Johanna and Jacoba Steenkamp and lives with them in an atmosphere of harshness and rigid self-control. Andrina, the young girl, is his natural child. He is ashamed of his past and cannot face up to it. Therefore his love for the girl is suppressed and twisted. Before the Englishman comes to Harmonie, he has no self-knowledge. He has not been conscious of the wall of self-righteousness between himself and Johanna, thinking it an evidence of his own power.

But now Andrina is growing older. Her breasts, of which she is so ashamed before her Aunt Johanna, are swelling. She is reaching womanhood. Aalst Vlokman is upset and tormented by this. He falls into a fit of anger when Johanna and Jacoba make a floral sacrament dress for Andrina, forcing the fact home to him that the girl is now a woman. Just as Andrina is growing up, Henry Nind comes to the district. Instinctively, Vlokman realises that the Englishman is wild and careless, a stranger who may lure his child to the very sin which he has committed himself. Andrina's attainment of maturity and the arrival of the Englishman force the beadle from his proud, isolated bitterness. He has to decide what he is going to do about Andrina and, at the same time, how he is going to face up to the past.

Now it is necessary for Vlokman to destroy the barriers which cut him off from the Steenkamp sisters and from his daughter. For the first time he realises how powerless he is to achieve this, and feels the real extent of his isolation. When he comes snooping round the Harmonie homestead garden to see if Andrina is safe from the Englishman, he comes up to her and "halted with no word to utter."⁹ Finally he speaks in words of rage, ill-expressing his concern. Andrina can only conclude that he is ill.

The beadle now tries to ensure that Andrina will be married off to one of the young bachelors in the Aangenaam Valley and thereby be out of harm's way. He offers his two precious plough oxen to Jan Beyers as a marriage portion for Andrina. He regards this as a sacrifice to the Lord, who will surely respond favourably. Yet he is not happy. Until the question of Andrina's marriage with Beyers is settled he cannot rest. Vlokman does not realise that without a resigned and accepting temperament there can be no peace of mind. So:

Everything pointed to the success of his scheme for saving Andrina from the Englishman, yet nothing brought him assurance.¹⁰

The church service for the examination of the young people who are to be admitted to the congregation shows how far Vlokman still is from the ideal state. In his address, the Pastor, Niklaas Joosten, stresses the love of God. "With God there was no forgetting, no failing in His care, no stinting of His mercy, no withdrawing of His love."¹¹ When Andrina bows in affirmation to the promises made on her behalf by the minister, and gentle Aunt Jacoba is moved to tears, the beadle sees nothing. He is too much twisted up in himself to appreciate the address or the act of his daughter.

Andrina refuses Jan Beyers, and, soon after, Aalst Vlokman hears from Betje Ferreira that the young man is to marry her granddaughter. He is so shocked that he has to clutch onto a spoke in the wheel of the wagon next to which they are talking. The old woman is very happy, convinced that it is the will of God. Unaware of the bargain the beadle has made, she tells him of this conviction: no one can escape the will of God, she says. This has the force almost of a challenge to him. Earlier the Pastor had implied that he could not escape the love of God; as Aalst Vlokman sees it at this stage, he will never be able to escape the vengeance of God.

His self-confidence is shaken. He feels defeated in his attempts to separate Andrina from Henry Nind. Already he has the fatalistic attitude which is later to develop into acceptance. When he sees the Englishman at the sacrament service he takes it as another sign that God has refused his sacrifice. After the service he gives vent to all his anguish and fears in the little cottage which he shares with the Steenkamp sisters. Sensing his weakness, granite-righteous Johanna challenges him to say what claim he has on Andrina:

"Make known your right to all the world and afterwards it will be for you to say what Andrina shall wear and whom she shall marry. But not till your right is known to all the world shall you say it!"[12]

Johanna makes crystal-clear what Aalst Vlokman has already begun to realise dimly for himself. He must come to terms with his own past if he is to have any real say in Andrina's life. There follows for the beadle a time of emptiness and chaotic thought. He feels he is mad to stay on at Harmonie while Johanna is gaining the upper hand in the house. Once he is tempted to run away to the Kalahari Desert, but has a sudden vision of Klaartje, Andrina's mother, the day she ran away with him in his wagon.

Andrina and Klaartje have much in common. Both Vlokman and the Pastor realise this. Moreover, the young girl has come to be in a similar kind of position to her mother. Klaartje worked in a coffee-house after she had left the beadle. Andrina's task is to make coffee in the van der Merwe household. Aalst Vlokman is working in the fields and feeling depressed when he thinks:

Mevrouw had taken her up to the homestead, when the Englishman's presence there made it but another coffee-house as dangerous to the girl as the coffee-house in Platkops dorp had proved to her mother.[13]

The fact that he thinks of this suggests that Andrina's problem and his own past are connected in his mind. In his mental gropings he comes to realise that self-righteousness is not such a good thing:

Righteousness with Johanna had proved a terrible weapon for evil.

If Johanna had but sinned a little she would have been a better woman. . . . But Johanna had never sinned. Thus she was damned.[14]

The old clear-cut borders between right and wrong, the sheep and the goats, are breaking down for Aalst Vlokman. He wonders if he thinks he is God or the Devil to want to save Andrina from sin while wishing that Johanna had sinned:

There was no reason in his thoughts. They led him nowhere. They ran through his mind like snakes through the grass—as mysterious in their coming as in their going. And life was like that. A slipping out of darkness into light and out of light into darkness again.[15]

Henry Nind tires of Andrina and of Harmonie and decides to leave. To his amazement the young woman does not try to hold him. She is sent to Cornelius's sheep farm in the Caroline district and runs away when Cornelius's wife discovers her to be pregnant. Aalst Vlokman is in agony about his daughter. At first he fears that she has gone to the Englishman; but even when he knows she is in the Caroline district he is tortured especially by the thought of men who "come in the night with wagons to steal young girls away."[16] Of course he is thinking again of his past.

Years of pride and self-righteousness are hard to eradicate. He still clings to his "right of service in the house of God."[17] Johanna has been receiving letters from Andrina, but refuses to tell him where and how she is. At last meek and forgiving Jacoba has a letter sent to her. In a bitter, exultant mood, Vlokman finds her in the orchard and hopes to know the news from Andrina. Then something in Jacoba's humility annoys him. He wishes to escape from her love, so that she will not have to forgive him any more. But Jacoba's love comes to seek him out. She offers to share the letter with him. This is the last straw. As he realises that he can never escape from his feeling of guilt towards Jacoba, he falls "to a riot of cruelty that came near to the madness so eagerly feared by Tan' Linda."[18] He turns on her, eyes blazing:

"Keep your letter to yourself, Jacoba Steenkamp," he said, moving deliberately away from her. "Keep your letter to yourself as Johanna has kept hers. What is Klaartje's child to me?"[19]

For a long time afterwards the beadle is filled with remorse for what he had done in this moment. Jacoba dies, and he cannot erase from his mind the picture of her shrinking from him as if she had been struck with a whip. It has taken this act to strip the last vestiges of pride and self-righteousness from him. When the Pastor is speaking about Jacoba at the thanksgiving service, Vlokman is moved to make a public confession. Standing alone on the wide stone step, he confesses that he is the father of Andrina and is responsible for Jacoba's death.

He, who was always ready to swing the blame upon others and to judge them, is now laying it upon his own shoulders. As a result, he must give up his old life in the Harmonie community. An official of the church, a man expected to set a public example, has proved himself the greatest of sinners. The beadle accepts his position, bitter as it is. He trudges away, turning round once to have a last look at the place he loved so much.

Now that he has confessed his sin, he feels that there can be no barriers between him and his daughter. He is no longer tormented by the thought of the Englishman. His jealousy and fear have been replaced mysteriously by indifference. Like Hans Rademeyer he is a wanderer, without a position in society. He has become humble, desiring only to work for Andrina and her child.

It is early spring when Aalst Vlokman, walking along the Cortes-dorp-Losberg road, sees Andrina's sacrament dress hung out on a bush to dry. He had hated this dress before, because it was a sign of his daughter's maturity. But now it is like a sign from the Lord. Hans Rademeyer comes round the corner of the house and the two men speak together, quietly, patiently, equals in spirit. The beadle waits alone while Hans Rademeyer goes into the house to talk to Andrina. He is now aware of the mystery in life, and it seems to him as if God has shown him the way by a series of miracles. At last he has been able to reconcile and accept the love, the wrath, and the justice of the Lord.

Aalst Vlokman wonders if Andrina will accept him. His fears are all centered on his own shortcomings, whereas before it was always the sins of others which concerned him. When he finally goes into the bedroom to see Andrina and her son, she says: "Come in then Ou-pa . . . and see the little grandson that you have, with his round bald head."[20]Aalst Vlokman who, at the beginning of the novel, had no man to call him friend, no child to call him Oom, has changed from a solitary, self-righteous man to one who accepts and does not judge. As a grandfather he is now part of a family, and through the confession of his sin is able to make known his relationship with Andrina.

The two Steenkamp sisters also illustrate Pauline Smith's interest in self-righteousness and forgiveness. Johanna is hard and unforgiving, but, unlike Vlokman, she undergoes no change. Even when Jacoba has died she does not drop the "wall of pride and righteousness behind which she guarded so jealously her shamed and stricken soul."[21] Right to the end she stays isolated and haughty. Even the Pastor, Niklaas Joosten, cannot penetrate her pride. Jacoba, on the other hand, is pliant and forgiving:

. . . in [her] gentle heart no bitterness could ever live, no sin remain unforgiven. Jacoba was never, like Johanna, roused to anger by the wickedness of others, but always gently amazed by their goodness.[22]

Sometimes she needs her sister's strength. When Johanna has bought the floral cloth at the Jew-woman's store, she has to get to work to cut it for the dress. Jacoba could never have brought herself to touch it. Yet, in the long run, it is the strength of her love and forgiveness, working even after her death, which moves Aalst Vlokman to confess that he is the father of Andrina.

Contrasted against the development of the novel's hero—the beadle—is the progress of Andrina, the young heroine. Aalst Vlokman's unconfessed sin haunts him, leaving his mind in a state of turmoil. Unlike him, Andrina is completely at one with herself and her surroundings. Even when she falls in love with the Englishman, her simplicity is not destroyed. Her love for Harry and her love for God become one in her mind. By loving him she does not grow selfish. Indeed she grows even more humble and generous towards others as her joy increases. Henry Nind misunderstands her. He thinks it is her mental courage and a will to be careless and rebellious which make her his lover.

In fact, she has accepted it as something given from outside herself.

> While the Englishman prided himself on being a free agent Andrina knew herself to be entirely in the hands of God.[23]

Andrina is tempted to judge Henry when he says he is leaving. With delicate art Pauline Smith shows how Andrina reviews in her mind her whole relationship with the Englishman and quickly comes to the conclusion that "In nothing had he deceived her."[24] She decides that this is a test of her love and that she must let him go. Her second temptation is to be jealous of the woman to whom Henry is returning, Lettice Featherstone. When Andrina goes up to the sheep farm in the Caroline district she is sorrowful because Harry is gone. Worse still is her jealousy. She feels that this was "in some way a betrayal of her love for the Englishman and the only evil thing which that love had brought her."[25]

When she knows that she is to have a child, she regains much of her calm. Moral Antoinette tells her that it is sin and shame, and this disturbs her so much that she asks old Hans Rademeyer what he thinks. His reply is central to Pauline Smith's concern with self-righteousness and resignation in this book.

> "Look now," he said at last, "for every sin there is pain, and for every sin there is sorrow. But when one comes at last through the pain and the sorrow to peace, surely that peace is the peace of God. Surely it is so, my child."[26]

This is a definition of sin which applies to the experience of both Andrina and Aalst Vlokman. The beadle has to realise that self-righteousness, pride, and judging others are sins because they bring him pain and sorrow. Andrina has to see that where there are no longer sorrow and pain, there can be no sin.

CHAPTER 7

"Desolation" and "The Father"

"DESOLATION" and "The Father" are given a separate chapter because they were written after Pauline Smith had made another trip to South Africa, and after the publication of both the first editions of *The Little Karoo* and *The Beadle*. The two stories were included in *The Little Karoo* when it was reissued in Jonathan Cape's "The Travellers' Library" in 1930.

I *"Desolation"*

In this short story, Pauline Smith has chosen a setting outside the large area focused on Platkops dorp which she had used for earlier work. Old Alie van Staden lives on the farm Koelkuil in the Verlatenheid, a district immediately to the north of the mountain range which divides the Little Karoo from the Great Karoo. As its Afrikaans name implies, the area is lonely and desolated, well-nigh a desert. Alie van Staden, who has lived most of her years in an environment like this, is strong and tenacious of life, yet accepting.

For just over three years there has been drought to the limit of their endurance. Much of Pauline Smith's interest lies in how her different characters bear up under these adverse conditions. They are a test of faith and spiritual qualities. Godlieb Bezedenhout, the ruined owner of the farm, and Stephan van Staden, Alie's son and a *bywoner* dying of tuberculosis, both begin to crack up. Stephan thinks that God is against him and begins to complain bitterly about his lot. Bezedenhout grows self-righteous and unreasonable. They are continually fighting with each other. Old Alie, who has learned the most from adversity, preserves her integrity best:

"Desolation" and "The Father"

> Sitting on the high stone step in front of the bijwoner's house, gazing in melancholy across the Verlatenheid, she would listen in silence to the arguments of both master and man alike.[1]

To Bezedenhout her silence is a judgment of himself. He has a guilty conscience because of his unjust treatment of the *by-woners*; but he cannot bring himself to admit his own fault and loads the blame onto Alie van Staden's shoulders. When Stephan finally dies he is relieved to think that he will now be able to get rid of the old woman. In the scene at the graveside Godlieb Bezedenhout's shallow self-justifications and petty selfishness show up pathetically against Alie van Staden's resignation and self-control. Her one thought is how she shall protect her grandson, Koos—the small orphan "with eyes as dark as her own, and long thin fingers like the claws of a bird."[2] He is wild and delicate, and there is a suggestion that his qualities can only be appreciated to the full by someone like Alie, who has known a harsh world demanding fortitude and self-abnegation. Now she must set out on the difficult journey to Hermansdorp, where she hopes to find the work which she had once done as a younger woman.

The description of the journey is one of the strongest pieces of Pauline Smith's writing. Sturdy realism, descriptions which are at once poetical symbols and matters of fact, and a moving, brooding compassion are all combined. The reader is told of the dry *kuils* or water-holes where the skeletons of dead sheep and donkeys lay, of the single pool, covered with slime, where the animals could get a little to drink, and finally of the donkeys touching her clothes with their parched tongues to find what moisture they could. The scene is factual and real, even down to minute details. At the same time there are descriptions which seem to show that this is a spiritual journey for the old woman and her grandson.

> The country ahead of them now was flat as a calm grey sea, its veld unbroken by any kopje until the long low line of Hermansdorp hills was reached. Yet in the shimmering heat of noon this sea became a strange fantastic world that slipped into being, vanished, and slipped into being again as they gazed upon it. Around them now were ridges of hills where no hills could be, banks of trees where no trees grew,

and water that was not water lying in sheets and lakes out of which rose strange dark islands and cliffs.[3]

This mirage landscape opens out before them not only as a physical reality but also as an alluring hint of a mysterious and wonderful world either within or outside of themselves which they can guess at but do not attain. One is reminded of Leonardo da Vinci's "Madonna of the Rocks" painting where the strange, intricate background of rocks and winding rivers help us to form an idea of the great spirituality in the Virgin. Also, the small poisonous bush "bright as a jewel in that desert of sand and stone,"[4] is like an evil temptation. Were old Alie to allow the animals to eat from it, they would die.

Descriptions make clear that the *bywoner* woman's memory has turned the Hermansdorp of her youth into a place more joyful and wonderful than real life. The "running furrows of clear water,"[5] the blossoming trees, the whitewashed church, and the gaol, which to her simple mind was like the heavenly house of many mansions—all these things suggest that the village has become the symbol for a perfect haven in her mind. Hermansdorp is a kind of New Jerusalem for Alie van Staden. Part of the sadness of the story is that, one by one, these beautiful images in her memory are shattered. The thorn-trees at the village dam are no longer laden with "the scented golden balls of spring"[6] but are stark and dry. The cypresses in the graveyard are no longer dark and slender as she remembered them, but a dull rusty brown. The furrows are dried up.

Even the small house where she had lived with Betje Ferreira is eluding her. Instead she comes to the orphanage and, realising she must provide for her grandson, boldly takes him into the ground where the children are playing. Koos is taken in by Justine de Jager, a young woman full of enthusiasm and energy. The orphanage can give the boy food and company. Although it is a bitter parting, it is right that he should be separated from his grandmother who is now near death, pain-ridden, beset by an old person's memories and visions.

As she walks back sorrowfully to her wagon, she does not hear or reply to a greeting from some women. It is a hard irony that at the time of her life when she feels most humble and dejected she is called proud by them. Sitting on her folding chair, she begins to remember the past, and Koos's face, "turned towards her in bewilderment and appeal"[7] rises in her imagination. The one thing which relieves the stark austerity of her dying is the illusory thought that she will find Tan' Betje's house and get work as a mattress maker.

Up some other lane it must be, but she would find it. A little house with green shutters and a pear-tree in the yard . . . buckets under the pear tree . . . and coir spread out in the sun.[8]

Up some other lane it must indeed be, because old Alie van Staden has been looking for a final home, which is beyond death. But that is not the main concern of the short story; the emphasis in character and action is on this world alone. Pauline Smith has tried to show the strange way in which Alie van Staden's memories of Hermansdorp could be transmuted in her mind. The tale is sombre, but not despairing. The reader is moved by a powerful, positive emotion when contemplating the austerity and bitter progress of the heroine's life. The plot does not iron out the frustrating dissonances and doubts of reality. Even though Alie has been lucky enough to find an orphanage where she can leave Koos, we do not know by the end of the story whether he will be allowed to stay there. Justine de Jager assumed that the old *bywoner* had a note from her Pastor when she admitted the boy. What attitude will Juffrouw Volkwijn take when she comes back? The possibility is that Alie's one success, in finding a home for the boy, may also have come to nothing.

II *"The Father"*

Piet Pienaar has a farm called Volharding, or Perseverance, in a poor, and for Pauline Smith's writing, new region of the Little Karoo. But a section of land which stands between him and the river belongs to the vast estate of harsh Meneer van Reenen already introduced in the story called "The Sinner." Pienaar is a man who has started with nothing. By dint of hard work and saving he has gradually built himself up to possess his land. For him power is everything. His one wish is to buy the land which Meneer van Reenen has let out to a poor relative of his wife, Oom Phanse. Then with his land bordering on the river the farm

. . . would be not a wedge in shape but a hammer—and with this hammer, and its water-rights, Piet was convinced that riches could be won . . . by the growing of Kombuis tobacco.[9]

It is clear that the hammer is a symbol of power. Piet Pienaar can only get on with other people by dominating them: "battle was to him the natural means of intercourse, with his fellow-men."[10] He had broken his wife's spirit to such an extent that she is reduced to lifeless passivity. For him marriage was a means of producing children to work for him. His attitude is to cash in on the fecundity of nature and make it enlarge his own pride and possessions. Unfortunately for him the processes of nature lie beyond his control, and his wife bears only one son, Klaas. For this he has never forgiven her nor God. To make matters worse he cannot touch or bind the essential personality of his son. Klaas is little better than a slave, working even at the age of twenty-seven as an unpaid labourer on his father's lands. Yet, whenever Piet wants to argue, provoking some definite response, the young man submits and so eludes him. He remains a stranger, something perpetually outside his father's influence.

When the drought hits the region, Piet is exultant because he thinks that the land will drop in value. He carefully prepares his scheme, telling Oom Phanse that the soil is worthless and persuading him to leave. Finally, when the old man decides to abandon the lands, Piet is ready to make his offer. The night before he is to drive to Meneer van Reenen he counts the money he has hoarded in the loft of his house. His mind is in a turmoil of exultation and anxiety. For the first time he feels the loneliness and distress which are the inevitable fruits of the life he has led:

. . . there came upon him unreasonably, without warning, with a sharp pricking in his spine that was like the ice-cold touch of an enemy creeping upon him from the rear, a sense of almost unendurable loneliness.[11]

As this feeling is upon him, he sees Aantje down below, driving the hens into their hock. He wants to call to her, but he cannot. Once again Pauline Smith is showing that deeds done in the past have a strangulating effect on the present.

Meneer van Reenen treats Piet harshly. Like the poorer farmer, he is ambitious and grasping, although he has a greater understanding of other people. He speaks in derision, telling Piet that he was a fool to think that he could get the lands so cheaply. In fact Meneer van Reenen has been following the whole progress of farming in the Magerplatz area. Piet Pienaar realises that "through all these years Mijnheer, giving no sign, had been watching him, playing with him."[12]

Piet has behaved as if life is only the survival of the fittest, and now he has been hoisted with his own petard. Pathetically, he stands before the rich, grim, cynical farmer. Piet plunges even further into isolation and resentment. Although life does not seem to be worth living, he does not think that he may have been in the wrong. Consequently, he misses an opportunity to mend his ways, and his attitude becomes more and more unrealistic as his jealousy grows. His imaginings of evil grow more wild. They "offered themselves to his mind like crazy guests but awaiting a welcome."[13] No longer does he see people for what they are. They become symbols playing out parts in his own fevered brain. In a telling description Pauline Smith shows how Piet has lost all contact with the world around him:

His brooding resentment found no relief in utterance except when sudden fury seized him and shook him into speech that seemed to his hearers to have no connection in time or place with the matter in hand.[14]

Now he hoards his evil suspicions as once he had hoarded his gold. Finally he comes upon the idea that Klaas is not his son. We are told that Meneer van Reenen knew Aantje in his wild youth, but it is not positively suggested that Klaas is his child. It is Piet's unreasonable jealousy and bitterness, described as an "evil phantasy,"[15] which suggest the idea to him, and it is very understandable; for in this way his grudges against God, Meneer van Reenen and Klaas can all be brought together in one being.

Finally, in his solitary madness, he determines to kill Klaas. His young son, and the new *bywoner* on Meneer van Reenen's land, Hendrick Mostert, have gone down to the river to look for a waterhole. Piet sets out after them with his gun. Suddenly Aantje realises what he is going to do. She runs across to the *byowner's* house to fetch Dientje, the young woman who has grown to be friendly with Klaas.

Again Piet Pienaar's inner world is completely out of keeping with his surroundings. He is lying in wait for his son when suddenly he feels a pressure at the back of his head, the "deadly grip of the unseen and inhuman enemy."[16] This is the terrifying experience of loneliness which had first assailed him when he was counting the money for the van Reenen lands. It is the utter nullity that lies at the end of his chosen course. Dientje runs after him, calling "Piet Pienaar! Piet Pienaar! What would you do then, Piet Pienaar?"[17] The words of the gentle compassionate woman are full of concern and urgency. But the farmer is now living entirely within the infernal region of his own brain. To him the words are spoken by an "inhuman presence."[18] They grow louder and louder until, turning in terror, he stumbles and shoots himself with his own gun. Like Andries Lombard, the miller, Piet Pienaar cannot make himself understood at the moment of his death. In life "he risked friendship with no man, and even from his wife and his son did he instinctively withhold his thoughts."[19] Now, while he is dying, no one can tell what is passing through his mind.

As the world grows more alien and meaningless for Piet Pienaar, it blossoms into new experience and richness for his son. Unlike his father, Klaas has a love of the land for its own sake and not only for the wealth which can be harvested from it.

The green of other men's lands was never so green to Piet as the green of his own, but Klaas had looked upon all alike with a clearer and juster vision.[20]

Klaas gives disinterested advice to Meneer van Reenen about the growing of Kombuis tobacco on Oom Phanse's land. The young man is compared to a willow branch, green and full of life, bowing beneath the sterile wind of his father's anger. He is seen as being in tune with the land,

> . . . moving slowly across the earth—tall and gaunt, a part of the rapidly greying landscape, drawn gently into it as he moved, held by it.[21]

Consequently, when the Mosterts arrive Klaas can appreciate them, warming to the gentle love of Dientje and responding to the enthusiasm and innocence of the children. Their arrival is the ruin of Piet Pienaar's plans, but for Klaas it provides an awakening into new experience. Klaas's growing love for Dientje is contrasted to the increasing bitterness and disillusion of his father's life. Unlike Piet, who habitually adopted an unthankful attitude to the joys or privileges of life, neither of the young people regard the new experience which comes to them as a right. Dientje has not refused to look after Hendrick Mostert's children because they are not her own. Klaas has never thought of marriage as a possibility for himself. In this story Pauline Smith has given another form of expression to one of her favourite themes—that miserliness, self-righteousness, and love of power lead to nothing, while an accepting and just state of mind can open up new love and closeness between people.

CHAPTER 8

"The Last Voyage" and "The Cart"

A SHORT story, "The Cart," and a one-act play, "The Last
Voyage," can be found amongst the typescript material
given to the library of the University of Cape Town about a
year after Pauline Smith's death in 1959. A little about the play
is to be gleaned from *A.B. . . . 'a minor marginal note,'*[1] where
Pauline Smith records that she wrote it after the short story
"Desolation." Therefore it comes in the period after 1927 and
seems to have been written before she started work on "The
Father." She mentions that the play did not satisfy Arnold
Bennett as much as the short stories. No mention is made of
"The Cart" in *A.B. . . . 'a minor marginal note,'* but we do know
that is was published in South Africa in 1925. Unlike the other
short stories which are collected in *The Little Karoo*, "The Cart"
is a humorous tale.

I *"The Last Voyage"*

In this play, which is set in Cape Town, John Tunstall, a
retired clerk of seventy-two, has to learn that it is not reasonable
to try and stave off death indefinitely, and that the love which
exists between him and his wife (and can exist between him
and his children) is worth as much as the chance of another few
years on earth. The old man has the idea that every voyage he
makes to England will add five years to his life. He has just
saved up another fifty pounds to pay his passage. In a soliloquy
he shows that it is fear of death which motivates him.

John (Whispering). Just enough for my passage in the old *Tro-*
jan . . . . Just enough . . . . no more . . . I can just manage it. (He

pauses, looking up across the room, at something unseen, in a slowly deepening horror; Whispering again) Death! . . . Death! How do people face it? To go out . . . into darkness . . . alone . . . alone.[2]

He cannot accept that now he is near death. The thought of gaining time obsesses him. The pernickety way in which he looks after the clock on the wall seems to suggest this. The unfortunate fact of his grandson's illness and the action of his wife, Susan, bring him to realise that he is being selfish and unrealistic in his attempts to prolong his life. Susan is "a quiet, gentle woman of 67, and, in spite of her poverty, still possesses charm."[3] Unlike her husband, she is loving, accepting, and concerned for the welfare of others. When John Tunstall asks peevishly for his milk she quietly leaves hers to one side to give to her grandson. The old man cannot bring himself to see the needs of others, just as he is unable to face up to the fact of his own approaching death.

Susan goes over the road to get a toy for Johnnie to play with. Soon after, Robert Barton, John's son-in-law, arrives to say that the boy will not be coming to visit. He has been having trouble with abscesses in the hip and is "worse than he's been yet."[4] It appears that the child will need another operation, and this can only be performed by Braithwaite, a surgeon from Port Elizabeth. His fee and fare will cost fifty pounds, which Barton cannot afford.

John (In a tone of horror) Fifty pounds! Where'll you get £50?

Barton (Awkwardly) That's what Nancy wanted me to see you about. She thought perhaps you might be able to lend us. . . .[5]

John Tunstall explodes and says he will not be able to lend the money. He cannot rise to the occasion and sacrifice his own voyage. Robert Barton is ill-at-ease while he is alone with his father-in-law. Tunstall's self-centredness and failure to accept make easy relations with others impossible. As soon as Susan returns he is more at home. "In his manner towards her there is both deference and tenderness. They understand each other."[6] Robert tells his story again and mentions the sum which is needed. There is a long, tense silence. "Susan is waiting for John to speak, but John does not speak."[7] He has had a second chance to overcome his selfishness, but again he cannot rise to the occasion.

Susan asks Barton if he will buy a bottle of Bovril for her husband's lunch on his way back to work. She tells John to pay for it, but he will not. At once she tackles him about the money for the boy's operation, but he will not listen, saying, "I'll not be sacrificed for Johnnie."[8] Her reply is harsh and to the point, stripping him of illusions and asking him to look squarely at the facts about himself and his grandson.

John, you're an old man now, and I'm an old woman. Whatever we do or don't do, the end must come soon for both of us. Our lives are nearly done. But Johnnie's is only begun. What would you sacrifice if you gave up your voyage for Johnnie? What does your voyage bring you, husband, that's so precious you can't give it up? Is it something dearer to you than Johnnie? Something that will still be dear to you if when you get back there is no Johnnie—or only a cripple Johnnie?[9]

Still he will not see. He minimizes his grandson's illness. "He's got through these attacks all right before and he'll get through this one all right now."[10] He will not be stopped because of Johnnie. Susan then appeals to his responsibility towards her. She tells him how his sea-journeys every five years have left her lonely and concerned in the past. He remains indifferent: "Don't be a fool, Susan. You wear me out with your talk. I tell you for the last time. I'm going."[11]

His wife realises that the only way he will learn is by being paid back in his own coin. She forces herself to become cold and indifferent, telling him she is going to live with Nancy. He will find his clothes prepared for the voyage.

Susan . . . The Bovril I'll take to Nancy. You say you don't need it, and Robert paid for it. It's Robert's. Not yours. You're a selfish old man, John. You would have let Robert pay for that Bovril just as you let Nancy pay for most of the things the doctor ordered for you when you were ill. All through these last five years Nancy and Robert have helped me to get things for you that you wouldn't pay for yourself. And all through these last five years you have been hoarding up money and hiding it away in the clock so that you might go off on another voyage. And why, John? Why? I'll tell you why—because once, years and years ago, old Nicolas Thornsen said a voyage added five

years to a man's life. Did you think I didn't know what your "business"—your "secret" was husband? Did you think I didn't know?
(Brokenly . . . .) You, John—an old, old man . . . letting Johnnie
die—because you want five more years to live . . .[12]

Susan has told him straight what she thinks of him, and he is
left alone and empty. At last he is brought to realise how much
he depends on her affection. Again he soliloquizes, revolving in
his mind the horror of death. But now he is as much concerned
that Susan has left him. He is staggered by her leaving him in
this way and realises how self-denying and loving she is. John
Tunstall is coming round to a better understanding of himself
and the people around him.

Suddenly for him, the struggle is over. The indifference of death,
though he does not recognise it, is upon him . . . he pulls himself
together with an effort, takes the bundle of notes out of his pocket
and puts it on the table.[13]

He has recognised Johnnie's claim to the money and, at the
same time, that he is old and near death. Almost at once Susan
returns, wearing a bonnet and with a tear-stained face. She
runs towards him, crying that she cannot leave him. He is the
one to whom she belongs. Although the grandson has the greater
claim to the money, John still has the primary place in her
affections; he is not disregarded as he fears he would be. To his
wife he says: "Take off your bonnet, Susan. And sit down. I want
to see you."[14] These words are significant; John is seeing her in
a fresh light. He has realised that she is independent of himself,
somebody outside whom he needs.

This play is not of the same standard as Pauline Smith's short
stories and novel. She writes in *A.B.* . . . 'a minor marginal note':

Knowing nothing of the technique of the theatre, and at times
appalled by my own presumption, I wrote, because I had always *seen*
it so, a one-act play called *The Last Voyage*.[15]

This lack of technique is apparent. There is too much reliance
on stage direction and too little of the characters get into the
dialogue. The lengthy descriptions could not be adequately

transformed into mime and action by the actors. For example, the following stage direction reads more like a passage in a short story than part of a play. It would be very difficult, if not impossible, to act.

(Susan puts the last stitches into the waistcoat. She is crying, but her tears are the unnoticed tears of old age, and when she wipes them away it is with a movement that seems but part of the action needed for the polishing of glasses.)[16]

Some of the dialogue is lifeless, and parts of John Tunstall's soliloquies clumsy. When Barton says, "Sorry I startled you, Guv'nor. You don't look very fit yet. Where's the Mater?"[17] he is talking more like a dusty character from the English "realistic" theatre than a live Capetonian. As a whole the play strikes the reader as an exercise in the type of theatre created by Bennett, Priestley and Galsworthy, with a setting which is South African only in name. When words like "biltong" occur, they do not harmonise and seem merely attempts at local colour. John Tunstall's soliloquy in which he expresses his fear of death has insufficient imaginative power to encompass the subject. The effect is commonplace and melodramatic.

Death! . . . Death! How do people face it? To go out . . . into darkness . . . alone . . . alone. What happens to us when we go? What meets us in that darkness . . . that silence . . . stiff . . . cold . . . and alone . . . alone.[18]

Robert Barton, father of the stricken boy, does not come to life under her pen like Aalst Vlokman or Andries Lombard. There is no vigour of imagination to give him a significance transcending his immediate problems. He remains a clerk in a store, complaining about his difficulties. Although occasional scenes have dramatic tension (e.g., the awkward silence on the stage while Susan waits for her husband to offer the fifty pounds) there is insufficient energy and movement for the play as a whole to be dramatically successful and enthralling. John Tunstall's internal struggle is not conveyed well in the soliloquies. Pauline Smith is handicapped by not being able to use description and author's comment, two of the most striking qualities of her style in *The Beadle* and *The Little Karoo*.

II *"The Cart"*

Although this short story is lighthearted and at times downright funny, it shows as great an understanding of the rustic characters of the Little Karoo as the more sombre tales. The authoress's knowledge of their clumsy, practical joking and down-to-earth humour matches her presentation of their faith and slow, self-searching ways. Koenraad, who is telling the story, and Arnoud Ferreira are two young men working in a store. First amongst their enemies is the Government sheep inspector who "thought himself surely the Governor-General of all the sheep in the Caroline district."[19] Arnoud has been having dealings with "a queer little Englishman, who was farming for his health."[20] The young Afrikaner decides that the Englishman needs a wife, and in order to court her successfully he must have a tent-cart. Consequently when the sheep inspector falls ill on a neighbouring farm, Koenraad and Arnoud resolve to gain possession of his cart and to play a practical joke on the detested man at the same time.

Pauline Smith's description of the sick inspector is realistic, rough, and humorous. Koenraad says:

"The sheep inspector lay on old Rijk Raubenheimer's bed groaning like a bull. I tell you, it was pleasant to hear him. The noise that he made was like music in our ears."[21]

Arnoud knows that the man has colic, but both of them pretend that he is dying. They play their practical joke ruthlessly. Arnoud's words are brutally concrete:

"Man!" said Arnoud, "that's how he looks to me also . . . a dying man . . . and the ground so hard that we can never get it dug . . ."[22]

For an hour, as a sort of poetic justice, they read to him from the little black book of sheep regulations with which he has plagued the surrounding farms. When Koenraad sees that his grandmother's *droppels,* or drops, are beginning to help the man, he begins to angle for his cart. Surely the sheep inspector will be saved, he says, if he has more *droppels*. But to get more of the medicine he must sell them the cart and the *droppels* will be part of the payment. With characteristic realism Pauline Smith observes that the sheep inspector could only whisper:

"When he saw us hesitating like that, the sheep inspector stopped in his groans and asked us in a whisper to save him. Surely now when he groaned so loud, he could have spoken aloud. But no. All the time that he thought he was dying he whispered."[23]

Once the two men get the cart they proceed to prepare it for the Englishman. Arnoud has a low opinion of the man's strength of character. Early in the story he says to him:

"It's a great pity they named you James. A man that's named James is bound to be a weak man. He can't help it. If they'd named you now Jimmy or Jim you might have been able to choose a wife for your-self. But surely as you are named James, you do right to come to Koenraad and me to choose her for you."[24]

The Englishman appears to find it very difficult to settle on a colour for his courting cart, and Koenraad and Arnoud have high jinks painting it different colours. At last they agree to paint it the colour of his wife-to-be's eyes. James asks Arnoud if he is sure that her eyes are blue. " 'I am that,' says Arnoud. 'Such a blue as there is not in the eyes of any other woman in Caroline.' "[25] James gives the young man a wry smile. Koenraad has been disturbed about him for some time. There were times when he would wonder "if the Englishman were playing with us just as we were playing with him."[26]

It is not until they are on the way to Lategan's farm where James is to be betrothed to the farmer's daughter, Alida, that the Englishman offers any hints of his real strength of character. He is very silent, opening "so quickly the camp gates on Lategan's farm that were fastened in a way that it took a man a long time to learn."[27] When they arrive, Arnoud orders Alida to marry James because "being a weak sort of man, having the name of James, he needs now such a woman as you to be his wife and make up his mind for him."[28] Alida says she will not. It soon

becomes apparent that her younger sister, Lenitje, and the Englishman are in love. Alida tells Arnoud that James can take care
of himself. Arnoud, however, will not admit to the state of his
own heart; perhaps he is not yet fully aware of it. He asks her
why she will not marry the Englishman. " 'Because,' says Alida,
'the man I marry must have a mind of his own, and even so I
must make it up for him.' "29

Amidst laughter and relief, Arnoud is at last brought to realise
that he loves Alida himself and that he has been tricked by
James. Like many comic situations, this story depends for its
effect on misunderstandings which come to a satisfactory conclusion. The object or symbol which gives unity to the episodes
is the cart. It becomes the two young men's possession when they
trick the sheep inspector into thinking that he is dying. By letting
them have fun with the cart and pretending to so much indecision
in his choice of colours, James leads Koenraad and Arnoud into
thinking that he is a weak-willed man. Finally, it is the cart which
carries Arnoud, all unknowing, to his bride. He says of himself
to Alida: "he thought he was bringing you a husband in the blue
tent-cart, but he didn't know it was THIS husband."30

The slow, country humour of this story can also be found in
conversations between the bucolic suitor, Jan Beyers, and Tan'
Linda de Neysen in *The Beadle*. It is unfortunate that this story
was not added to one of the editions of *The Little Karoo*. Pauline
Smith's humorous writing is as important a part of her work as
her vision of forceful passions. "The Cart" would have added
variety to the uniformly sombre volume.

CHAPTER 9

An Important South African Journal

IN THE LIBRARY of the University of Cape Town is a bulky typescript of a *South African Journal* kept by Pauline Smith during a long holiday in the Cape. It was sent to this country together with some other manuscripts by Mrs. N. Cundall, a friend of the authoress in England, because she felt it would be in accordance with Pauline Smith's wishes. The journal is clipped into sixteen bundles and divided into sub-sections. Each bundle is numbered in Roman numerals on the cover and page numbers are pencilled in.

The first entry was made on Sunday, August 17, 1913. For just over nine months, with the exception of a few short breaks, she describes the people and places she visited, recording stories which appealed to her and her reactions to contemporary problems. The last instalment was completed on May 23, 1914. Undoubtedly she was keeping the journal with the intention of collecting material for later work. In one part she writes. "I've not taken the time to re-read and correct or make literary any of this diary—only write it as A. said, to refer to when I get home."[1] She was fortunate in meeting a number of people and in hearing certain tales which obviously form the inspiration for characters, atmospheres, and plots in *The Little Karoo* and *The Beadle*.

The *South African Journal* is also of autobiographical interest. In its pages the reader can form some understanding of Pauline Smith's attitude to religion and social problems, and catch many glimpses of her direct, simple, and generous character. Her style is easy and conversational. The journal is not only a source of possible ideas for her future literary work but also a day-by-day record of her journeyings which she posted in batches to her sister Dorothy, and brother-in-law, Alex Webster.

Above all, she shows herself to be interested in people—what they do, how they look, the things which they have felt and hoped. Everyone she meets is treated with the same austere but compassionate truthfulness. It is this ability to be so fair and tolerant to the people she meets in life which gives strength to her characterisation. Her attitude to the English and Afrikaans colonial South Africans is not simple. Although she admires their good points, she will not ignore their parochialism, prejudices, and tendency to take the line of least resistance. She writes.

As far as I can see just now the country is possessed by a generation in its transition stage, and that is always a troubled time. In this district wealth has come so suddenly and so easily to colonials, Dutch and English alike, the most of them have lost their heads. The English all have motor-cars, and the Dutch who don't have cars have all got rubber tyres to their cart-wheels "say the Stigmanns" and ease is all they think of. Their education has only just begun, among the Dutch I mean, and they will have to soak and season in it for several generations yet before they can use it to any good purpose.[2]

She distrusted especially the English people's feeling that they were superior to the Afrikaners. In her opinion they had no grounds for thinking this. Generally she finds them less interesting than the Afrikaans farmers. Pauline Smith understands the state of her own sympathies very well, recording how a shocked English settler told her that John Schoemann, the owner of Vlakteplatz (a farm where she had stayed for some time) had been imprisoned for aiding the Boers during the Anglo-Boer war. Her comment on this is:

Pauline quite unaware of this had been very sympathetic with the Dutch all her visit there, as she can't help being, and guesses old John thinks her a "pro-Boer" at heart, and fears X and Z (two English South Africans) would be in an apoplexy if they guessed it![3]

The humour of the passage and the light satirical thrusts at the outraged "colonial" are quite unmistakable. Despite her feeling of closeness to the poor, isolated Afrikaners of the Little Karoo and her appreciation of their simplicity and honesty, her view of them is not one-sided or idealised. In a long passage she tries to sketch their strengths and weaknesses as she sees them:

Apart from his language, his "taal" (which is not the Dutch, or the French, of his forefathers), the Dutchman seems to have no historic sense whatever except *grudges*. He will remember a grudge for generations, against a family or a nation, but in the history of his people apart from that—of their buildings, their homesteads and tree plantings, of their wanderings, his interest is of the vaguest. All the old houses have passed out of the hands of the original families, the sense of beauty which the people who built them had seems to have been utterly lost by the present generation. They have now no literature, no art, no architecture of any kind. If they have a passion at all it is to get the better of the English. And yet individually they are the most hospitable people in the world, giving a stranger, Englishman though he may be, a welcome as simple and sincere as Sarah's to the angels. In his house you are the Dutchman's guest and so long as you are his guest, grudges against your nation are forgotten. He will do far more for an English guest, always with the simplicity of the Old Testament fathers, than an Englishman would do for one of his own people. Hospitality is as natural to him as sleeping in his trousers, and quite without any monetary value.[4]

On another occasion she writes:

I don't know a people who have at once so much simplicity and sincerity, and beauty through this, and so much cunning and suspicion. I suppose it is that they are still uncivilized enough for both sides to show up so clearly as to appear startling. And I think more and more that there is a wonderful likeness between them and the Russian peasants, and a most awful difference.[5]

Although she admires the Bible for its simplicity and strong imaginative symbolism, she cannot believe in the literal truth of some of its stories. She records a conversation with Miss Julia Morris, a friend of hers in Oudtshoorn, in which they had differed about the Eden story. Pauline Smith comments:

It is no good explaining to her that the story of Adam and Eve is quite as true for me in a way as it is literally for her. She thinks I am only the "most frivolous person she has ever met!"[6]

She also found it difficult to accept the divinity of Christ. In her journal she recounts a talk she had with Thys Taute on her second inspiring visit to his farm, Mill River, near Oudtshoorn. Thys explains that he finds it difficult to talk to the Dutch Reformed Pastor about religion. He says:

"Lord P . . . I can't talk to him like I talk to you. He would be horrified. Look now how it is. Some people we can never tell our inmost thoughts to, however old our friendship may be and others—well,—my wife is a good woman—too good you know. She can believe everything in the Bible just as she reads it—I now again I can't. When my brother lay dying he said to me 'Thys—what now will become of me?' And I tell you I could say nothing to him but if there were a God he would understand and make allowances. I could not tell him that I have never been able to believe in Christ myself. And I tell you P. I cannot bring myself to take Communion—because of that."[7]

Her comment is:

Sitting round that fire we got to feel I think like two sinners shut out of Heaven by the predikant (minister). If the predikant would preach the humanity of Christ, not the Divinity, take him for a peasant teacher instead of the Son of God, perhaps they would do more for sinners like Thys and me and most of the rest of the world.[8]

Her notion of the humanity of Christ was closely related to her idea of him as a member of the poorer class in society—and this provides a link between her religious skepticism and her tendency to support the working classes in politics. In section six of the journal she tells us how she crossed swords with a medical doctor in George who was an ardent imperialist. She felt he was priggish and hypocritical. Christ is described as a social reformer in a passage following on a discussion with a staunch Anglican churchman who was lamenting that there were fewer *gentlemen*—the old public school and Oxford men—taking Orders.

I wanted to say that the head of the church was a tradesman's son and the biggest democrat of all, and I guessed he'd be pretty scandalised now if he could see the Church he is supposed to have founded, but I was afraid of getting too hot and saying too much. Anyway *He* was all for the poor—sinners tradesmen and dissenters from the synagogues—the rich young man who was no doubt public school and Oxford of those days, got the hardest answer of them all.[9]

Arnold Bennett had begun to widen Pauline Smith's reading from the time of their first meeting, introducing her to the work of modern authors. From the journal the reader gets a good idea of the writers who were interesting her at this time. On her journey up the coast from George she is reading Dostoyevsky. With this author in mind she comes to Plettenberg Bay, a small coastal resort, where she hears of a mad girl called Molly. Molly apparently was subject to some kind of epileptic seizure which was like a fire burning inside her. At these times she was compelled to fly out at somebody else or run like the wind or it would kill her. Pauline Smith records:

We saw Molly later, a very pretty girl, slight, very pale, very sad. She had come in from gathering Almond Blossom. Her face and her story haunted us for days after that. And as I was reading "The Idiot" at the time Molly's madness interested me intensely. In some ways it was accepted as simply as Dostoyevsky accepts Mishkin's.[10]

Also at Plettenberg Bay is Mr. Jones, "a very small old man of 80—almost a dwarf—with short legs slightly bowed, and a very round protuberant tummy."[11] She feels that Dickens would have been thrilled to have seen him. While Pauline Smith is making her first visit to Mill River Farm she is thinking about another prominent Russian author. She records that she spoke of Tolstoy with Thys Taute. Two modern English authors in her mind are H. G. Wells and, in particular, her literary "master," Arnold Bennett. A lady artist she meets in Cape Town reminds her of Mrs. Reach Haslam in The Honeymoon, one of Bennett's comedies.

In the South African Journal there is a suggestion that Pauline Smith is beginning to understand that her imagination is fired mainly by the country parts of the Little Karoo, by the farmers and bywoners who lived there. She writes that she would like to do a series of sketches on a number of country and bywoner boys and girls, contrasting them against the children of the townspeople. On these she comments humorously: "The little

Snows, Edmeadeses and Krauses, though all dears and my very good friends don't make "copy" like the others at all."[12]

Although she travelled widely in the Western Cape in the period recorded by the journal, most of the characters and stories which are to appear later in her writing come from the Little Karoo area. In particular, her visits to the farms Kruis River, Vlakteplatz, and Mill River are rich in source material. It is to be hoped someone will one day put out an edition of Pauline Smith's 1913-14 *South African Journal* so that it can become known to many of her readers. Certainly a selection from the sections which contain the bulk of the source material for her writing will be a valuable addition to her printed work. The following are extracts from the journal. They illustrate how Pauline Smith drew heavily on what she heard for some of the stories in *The Little Karoo*, and how she combined and modified her material for *The Beadle*.

I   *"The Pain"*

The idea for this short story came from a tale she was told. On December 16, 1913 (a holiday in South Africa to commemorate the victory of a group of Voortekkers over overwhelming odds of Zulu *impis* in Natal), she was watching the farmers ride into Oudtshoorn for the thanksgiving service at the Dutch Reformed Church. She was disappointed because the ceremony was less colourful than it had been in the past. Also there were no farmers with *takhaar,* or long hair. This reminded her of a story she had been told. She records the episode in her own words.

No Tak Haar Boer either and that reminds me of the Tak Haar who brought his wife into hospital. They were a very devoted couple and never slept apart till she had to have this operation, so, to be as near her as possible, the old man (Tak Haar means long uncut hair) pitched a tent on the veldt outside the hospital gates and lived there six weeks till he was able to take his wife home. It was winter time, and cold wet weather, but the old man refused to go in the town as that was too far from his wife.[13]

In "The Pain" she has elaborated this story considerably. There are other short stories like "Ludovitje" and "Anna's Marriage" where she is much more dependent on her narrative source in the journal. "The Pain," however, is interesting because it includes ideas from other sources as well. A month before the thanksgiving service on December 16 she must have got a hint for the character of Juriaan van Royen and his relationship with his wife when she travelled to De Hoop to meet Ou-Pa Lategan. The old man and his wife had been married for sixty years and lived in a house with an orchard nearby. While Pauline Smith was there, Ou-Pa went into the orchard and picked fruit for her. After the visit she wrote:

. . . the nicest bit was seeing the old Ou-Pa Lategan. I wish I could describe him better. There was so much nobility and simplicity in him, the kind of nobility and simplicity that you get in Russian literature.[14]

Her description of Ou-Pa Lategan's wife bears interesting resemblances (and differences) to that of Deltje van Royen:

The old lady grown childish, with such a pretty pink and white complexion, contradicting her toothless old mouth! She does little but cry, and has one eye with a fallen lid, wears her head in a sort of cloak and dresses in black calico.[15]

The idea for the peach-stone floor in the van Royens' cottage must have come from a third source—a story told to Pauline Smith by Kathie Taute on her second visit to the Mill River farm in the Langkloof.

Kathie speaking of the Kamanassie people on our return told us of a visit she once paid to an old lady there, very poor, whose forehouse was floored with *peach stones*. The peach stones all put into the mud floor like little cobbles, and worn, when Kathie saw it, to a polished smoothness with passing feet.[16]

II *The Beadle*

Descriptions and incidents which are later to be embodied in *The Beadle* can be found in Pauline Smith's *South African Journal* mainly during her two visits to the farm at Mill River in the Langkloof and on her expeditions to Vlakteplatz and De Hoop. In October 1913, she spent six days at Mill River. This place provides the setting, atmosphere and some of the characters for *The Beadle*. From the journal it is apparent that Thys Taute's farmhouse is the original of the Harmonie homestead. Like Harmonie, Mill River has a large, attractive kitchen. On the table is

. . . a beautiful old jam-pot, copper, with a lid the shape of a huge fish-kettle on a low brass stand brought by Mrs. Taute's Huguenot great-great-great-grandparents from France.[17]

This is to become the copper jam-pot "shaped like a huge fish-kettle"[18] mentioned in *The Beadle*. The reader is also told in the novel that it stood on a brass-stand "brought out from Holland by the first van der Merwe, who, as a Landrost in the service of the Dutch East India Company, had settled at the Cape."[19] Next to the Mill River farmhouse is a garden,

. . . at present a blaze of roses, 210 bushes all in full bloom. A yellow banksia just a shower of gold in one corner, a shower of lavender over the arch of wistaria. Ramblers over the arches and all down the old wall overlooking the old mill dam. A little sluit runs through the garden with mountain water. At one end of the rose terrace is the ruin of the old school-room and bedroom.[20]

This garden, the mountain stream and the schoolroom are to play important parts in *The Beadle*.

While Pauline Smith was at the farm, a man came in to say that his baby was ill.

The baby, 11 months old, had had convulsions the previous night and did not seem at all well this afternoon he said. It was suggested at once that Mrs. Taute should go over with the box and the book to see the child for herself. As the nearest doctor is 5 hours away they turn naturally to their neighbours for help, and Mrs. Taute seems here the medical adviser. . . . She got up from table, put on her hat and veil, and set off carrying the book and a small brass-bound medicine chest.[21]

This episode surely gives rise to that in *The Beadle* when Mevrouw van der Merwe, renowned throughout the Harmonie district for her medical skill, goes out to see what she can do to help Cornelia Mostert, the young daughter of a *bywoner*.

The authoress's second visit to this farm, in April 1914, provides her with more inspiration for Harmonie. Tan' Linda de Neysen's post office has its original in "a small, mud-floored room with a half-door, a big table, a pigeon hole and harness on the walls."[22] Here, with Mrs. Taute as post-mistress, "parcels are constantly being returned because insufficiently stamped."[23] Pauline Smith comments:

. . . and as the weights of the weighing machine are made up of odds and ends, pennies, etc. I don't wonder she is not always correct in her charges![24]

Near the Mill River homestead was a little shop where Pauline Smith and Mrs. Taute went visiting after tea. "It is kept by a very talkative Jewish woman, her son, and an assistant."[25] Esther Shokolowsky of "The Miller" and *The Beadle* was born in her imagination that afternoon. During this stay she accompanied Thys Taute when he went to the mill to fetch the miller's thank-offering for the thanksgiving service. She describes him:

Thys called out to hurry, but the old man, who looks about 80, and is I think just about 40, but dying of consumption, refused to partly through ill-health and partly through obstinacy. . . . His illness he says, caused by grinding the corn which makes him cough. He is as striking looking as ever with his dark mysterious eyes in his very white-grey face. Thys asked if they were coming to the Dank Feast. The miller gave a wheezy laugh and said, No he could not afford to go to the Dank Feast.[26]

Here, together with short descriptions made during her first visit to Mill River, are the first glimpses of Andries Lombard of "The Miller" and *The Beadle*.

At this time Thys Taute was preparing for Mill River's annual thanksgiving *Nagmaal*, a communion service which would be attended by all the members of his community. This was an event which seized Pauline Smith's imagination and moved her most deeply. She writes of it:

I was very glad indeed we had stopped on for this, for the whole thing touched me very much and seemed to me very beautiful in its simpleness and sincerity. Through it I got back to the old feeling for Nachtmaal Dank Feast that I remember as a child and that still holds people like Mimi and Niccoline Johanna. It is only here and there that one gets at it now, and it's that that I must write about if ever I can.[27]

She further describes how she went down from the homestead to the church to attend the festival:

We walked down in the sunshine, ostriches around us through the open werf, and down below us the little grey church which looks always so new and *cold,* and damp though it was built over 30 years ago.[28]

In *The Beadle* and "The Miller" this church has been changed by her imagination, becoming square and whitewashed.
The people had all arrived and the service began.

For a few moments it was all very still, and I found myself quite suddenly and foolishly on the verge of tears. It was such a beautiful morning. These people had come, many of them, from such long distances. Most of them were *very* poor. All were struggling at this time against horse-sickness, the most serious trouble the poor farmer has to face, and the slump in ostrich feathers. In this Long Kloof the folk are still so poor, so far away from the rest of the world that even the one motor car seemed unable to bring any outside element to disturb the sincerity, solemnity, beauty, what you will, of this little company of people drawn together to praise God with their harvest thanksgiving. The smoke from the fire by the wall going up straight in the clear air, was like a burnt sacrifice to Heaven. . . . The predikant then gave his address, very short, very earnest, very simple—to give the Lord of our fruits of the earth, to come together not only to praise him but to help one another. . . . He then "gave out" a hymn, starting it himself.[29]

A thanksgiving service of this kind, obviously so important a part of her inspiration, forms a high point in both "The Miller" and *The Beadle*. During such a service Andries Lombard tries to become reconciled to his wife and Aalst Vlokman is moved to confess his past.

If Mill River provides ideas for a setting and certain incidents, the farm Vlakteplatz on the bank of the Olifants River about thirty-two miles from Oudtshoorn contributes to the quiet, orderly atmosphere of Harmonie and to the serenity of its characters. Of the family who owned the farm she writes:

They were so sincere and solemn and gentle and good. And I was so worked up by it all. Their goodness and simplicity. The awful feeling that somehow and quite unintentionally I had taken them in, that I wasn't at all the good quiet person they imagined, that I ought to get up and confess my sin right away and get back to the place where I really belong.[30]

Mrs. Schoemann in particular impressed Pauline Smith. It is her serenity and spirit of acceptance which go into the character of Alida van der Merwe.

Strangely enough, although Mill River provides such a strong setting for *The Beadle*, the experience which touched off its plot and gave hints for Aalst Vlokman and the Steenkamp sisters came to Pauline Smith on a short visit to De Hoop. Here she met the Terblanches, old friends and patients of her father. She went down into their land to see Tan' Nellie and Tan' Betje "two old women who live in a little reed and mud hut."[31] Pauline Smith writes:

When we arrived Tan' Nellie was all alone. Tan' Betje very shy never appeared at all, but was, we think, engaged in making the coffee in the Rondavel kitchen across the yard. The little hut has 3 rooms, a forehouse with a half-door to the east, and a little hole for a window to the west, and an open space as door to the bedroom of Tan' Nellie and Tan' Betje to the south, and a second open space, hung with a clean white tablecloth, to a bedroom to the north where the Koster (Church Beadle) sleeps and has slept for years! He was once, many years ago, engaged to either Tan' Nellie or Tan' Betje, difficult to say which, when some objection was raised, and instead of marrying *one* sister he came to live with both and has lived with both ever since treating them as a rule very harshly.[32]

III *"Ludovitje" and "Anna's Marriage"*

In August 1913 Pauline Smith visited Mimi Bergh and her

husband on their farm at Kruis River East. This lonely place, lying near the foothills of the Outeniqua and Swartberg Mountains, charmed her. She was especially interested in Mimi, a heavily built, naïve Boer woman with a strong religious leaning and a tendency towards sadness.

The Berghs told her of the death of their youngest child, Pieterkie and of the special grave which they had dug for him. The following extracts show how closely Pauline Smith drew on the journal for the story which was to be called "Ludovitje." She reproduces as closely as she can the way in which Mimi and the farmer spoke.

Mimi took us up to Pieter's grave on the hill across the line. You look up to the white tombstone from our bedroom window. Pieter is the first of this family to be buried there. The old graves are down nearer the river. Mimi speaks of him very often. ". . . and how wonderful it was—the day that he died, that morning there came here a mason. We got him to dig now Pieterkie's grave. It took him now nearly the whole day to make Pieterkie's grave—that evening and the next morning as well—and it is all in the solid rock. Look now here—in those other graves that Mr. Bergh had dug out that same time. For one cannot get always a mason who can work. I mean we can only get workmen who are passing through on the tramp. So it is best to be ready. So we had these other graves also now begun, (four of them all pegged out and one left open, empty, and ready for the next to need it) then when the day come that we need it it is now ready. And now just let me tell you how nice we made that grave of little Pieterkie. We did make it very narrow at the bottom, narrower than the coffin. Then a little way up we did make it wider and put planks across, and on the planks we did rest the coffin and a little way above the coffin we did put zinc sheeting and then the ground above that again. So Pieterkie he live there like in a little room, and we did cement it also, nice and clean like a bathroom, and he lie there. . . . And every Sunday I do bring flowers for his grave and rest here, so peaceful and quiet. And these shells, you see them? Pieterkie did thread them on wire for his ou pa's grave and now they lie here on his. And look now on the tombstone we did carve the hymn that Pieterkie did sing on that day he lay dying. All day he sang it, and now you can read it here."[33]

The following sunday the Berghs took their guest with them to Pieterkie's grave. She records:

This was a very sad day, full of Pieterkie. It began in the morning after breakfast when Mimi took us down to her garden to gather flowers for the graves, daffodils, violets, roses, pig-lilies and Cape May. She spoke to us of his death. He died of diphtheria after I think only three days of illness. And showed me the little garden he had planted behind the orange trees is [?] her own. His favourite flower was periwinkle, and she took a lot of that out of his own garden for the grave. Then we went up the hill. Bergh, Mimi, A. J. and I with the flowers and Solomon the Indian with pails of water. All the time the talk was of Pieterkie, Pieterkie—and death.[34]

"Ludovitje" is perhaps the most Biblical in tone of all Pauline Smith's stories. One is not surprised to read that when she was staying at Kruis River East, Bergh struck her as an Old Testament sort of figure. "Bergh himself seldom uses a single word when a sentence can be utilised instead. Bergh is so big and well-fed looking and prosperous, so sure of himself in a heavy biblical way, so *pompous* . . . and in his kindness to others always biblical too."[35] It is very likely that with this farmer in mind she created the character of Piet, Ludovitje's father.

Bergh explained again how Pieterkie's grave was all cemented out and clean like a little room, and how all the other graves were dug out and filled only with loose gravel which could easily be removed when necessary. "People think it now strange of us to have the graves ready, but what is it? We must all die, and we know we must and I now am glad to think if I die suddenly my place is ready for me here by the side of my little Pieterkie."[36]

Later he told Pauline Smith about the boy's character and death.

To all outsiders Pieterkie was "soft" or "queer" and not quite right in his head. To Bergh and Mimi and the other children he was always something strange and heavenly. . . . He was a very religious little boy, and Bergh is very proud of his influence among the Kaffirs. The green or raw Kaffirs who came down to build his dam. Some of them were Christians, but most were not, and Pieterkie was very much distressed by this and did his best to convert them. Always after their work was done the Kaffirs came down to the house for their food and sat on the parapet wall above the railway line at the back of the house, and Pieterkie would go and sit with them and talk to them of heavenly matters, trying to convince them of the existence of his God. There was one man in particular whom Pieterkie had set his heart upon "saving." With this man he argued day after day without success. Then one evening while Bergh and Mimi were sitting out on the stoep Pieterkie rushed round to them like a mad thing, flinging up his cap and dancing and screaming in Dutch "It is a pearl in my crown. It is a pearl in my crown!"

They ran round to the back of the house again after him and found the Kaffir converted. No argument of priest or parson had convinced him, he said, of a God, but seeing how the spirit of the white man's God worked in the heart of a little child, that had convinced him.[37]

The boy's father was so moved by his son's influence on the Africans that he sent a number of Bibles to the Knysna wood-cutters, a poor and backward people living in the coastal forests. In these were pasted photographs of the dead Pieterkie and a short story of his life. Pauline Smith records:

(Bergh) told me also of his death. How on the last of the 3 days that he was ill Heyns or Raubenheimer came out to see him and said that he was getting better. As he left the room Pieterkie turned to the white "help" who was with him and said "He says that but he does not know what *I* know. Tonight I shall see my King." And he began singing his favourite hymn. That afternoon many people came to see him and his teacher asked him should she sing? And she sang to him and all the people in the room. The schoolchildren and all the farmers from round about sang with her. And when she stopped Pieterkie cried out "Look, look, a dove in the window has come for me." And we looked and saw nothing and presently he cries out again. "Another dove, another dove the Lord has sent for me. I come Lord Jesus. I come I come" and so he died.[38]

A comparison between these extracts and "Ludovitje" will show how much Pauline Smith is indebted to Mimi's story. It is inter-esting to note that on an earlier visit she had made an impression on the young Pieterkie, and that he evidently had a special place for her in his memory. This may have been an added stimulus to write the story. She writes: "He was fond of me as a child when I was out last, and they say used to talk of me very often, especially when gathering flowers. Always in the yellow buttercup daisy time he would gather the daisy and run up and hold it under Mimi's chin and say 'Let me see now like Tante Polly if you like butter. Yes you like butter. When Tante Polly comes again I will tell her.' "[39]

Mimi Bergh also told Pauline of the death of her sister, Kitty. This provided material for another story, "Anna's Marriage." Again the reader will notice that she has drawn heavily on her source.

At dinner (Bergh not present) Mimi spoke of Kitty's death—Kitty married young Rex against the wishes of the Leroux family. "When it was said that she would marry him, she came to see me, and I took her into your room and spoke ever so nicely to her and asked her did she know now this thing she was doing? and I tried to make her see the truth about him. We all knew it but she did not, and would not believe it, and she left me and she married Rex. And by and by it all so happened as we had known it would happen. Rex he got in money trouble and we all knew it but Kitty did not. He did pass bonds on the lands (Kitty's lands) and make debts and when the bonds debts get in the papers, then the papers were lost or something and Kitty did not see them. And we and her brothers thought Kitty must know—it is in the papers. But she never see those papers. He kept them all from her. And by and by it came that the creditors would make Rex bankrupt. And still Kitty did not know. And one day there came a man to the house and Rex told Kitty it was now a friend that would like to see the house and Kitty must take him all over the house and make him coffee. And Kitty did so and afterwards the man sat on the stoep writing."[40]

In her own story, Pauline Smith builds up the pathos of the man going round the house by showing how fond Anna was of her furniture. She also introduces the little black box which plays music as an indication of Philip's hold over her and of the dream-world in which she lives.

"And Kitty did not know it, but the man was now making a list of all the things that had now to be sold. All the furniture and the cattle and the lands and everything that was theirs. It was to be at the toll-house, the sale. But so quiet so quiet had Rex been that not one of my brothers knew that there was to be a sale. And the day of the sale, early in the morning Rex sent the boys with the cattle and horses and ostriches for the sale to the toll-house, and when coffee time came and Kitty asked now where were the boys Rex he say yes they have all gone off and he must now ride after them and fetch them back from the toll-house where they had gone for forage or something. And then there came the Jew man that was to have the sale and talk with Rex at the gate. And while they stand there my brother Gert rode past on his horse riding home. . . . And when he passed there Rex and the Jew man were talking talking. And Rex did not even look at my brother. And Rex and the Jew they talked harder than ever, and the Jew got angry and call out to my brother who was already past them. And first my brother Gert would not turn, but afterwards he turn and ride back to them and the Jew ask him if he had heard about the sale. And that was the first my brother heard of the sale and the bankruptcy."[41]

Pauline Smith makes use of most of this long, rambling tale. She eliminates the ineptitudes in Mimi's storytelling, but the Jew remains, as do such details as the cattle, the horses, and the forage. It is instructive to notice how she seizes upon the central situation in the account and magnifies it to the exclusion of other strands. Mimi had much to say about the subsequent feud between Stephan and Kitty's other brothers, when the former had come to a dishonest and separate agreement with the Jew about Kitty's property. In "Anna's Marriage" all the brothers act in complete accord in their desire to get the Brandwacht lands back into the family. According to Mimi, Kitty did not go mad in the house after it had been sold but went to stay with her mother. Later Rex approached her again with papers calculated to double-cross Stephan. When he asked her to sign them "Kitty faint away like as if her heart was broken, and they carry her through to my mother's room, and the next day Kitty was dead."[42] The journal reader is told that Kitty was more or less in poor health for some time. These subsequent events are suppressed by Pauline Smith. She takes the hint of Kitty's nervous condition and turns it into a state of madness which in the story follows directly and dramatically upon Philip's act of treachery. It is certain that the following passage provided Pauline Smith with the idea for the conclusion of the story. Mimi is describing what happened on the day of the sale and afterwards:

"*And Kitty was ill all that day and the next day, all alone in the house,* but my brother Hans sent his wife to see how she was. And my brother Hans wife see how ill she is and the next day she send for my mother, and that is the first my mother heard of Kitty's illness and the sale. And my mother take Kitty straight home with her in the cart [italics mine]."[43]

Comparing the journal and the final story may be of help to would-be writers. Here they can see what parts of an anecdote are essential, how they ought to be dramatised and highlighted, and how other things should be suggested or glossed over. They can learn how simplicity may be suggested without boredom, and naïveness without sentimentality.

Pauline Smith gained other information for her stories and novel at Kruis River East. She learned how Bergh allowed the *bywoners* to grow his tobacco for him, and how the plants were grown and the leaves dried and prepared. This knowledge is employed in "The Sinner" and "The Father." Possibly in Bergh there is a hint for the unyielding Meneer van Reenen of these stories.

IV   *"The Miller"*

In a section of this chapter devoted to *The Beadle*, the reader has been introduced to the original of Andries Lombard, the harsh-minded consumptive miller. Pauline Smith relates a discovery which Thys Taute, the master of the Mill River farm, had made concerning him.

Thys not long ago made enquiries about the land which the miller farms on his own as part payment for his work at the mill. He found that he had refused to plant his potato-land because he said to Doeri (his wife), "By the time it is time to dig the potatoes I will be dead of this cough that I have from the mill dust, and surely the day I am buried they will turn you out of the house, and the man who comes after me will dig my potatoes and eat them for nothing, so I will not now plant them. Be sure," he said, "that when I am dead they will do so to you the day I am buried, give our house to another and our potatoes also. Therefore I will not plant me my potatoes and God help you Doeri when I am dead and they turn you out of the house now to the veldt when I am buried."[44]

In the journal this story is used as an illustration of how suspicious the poor Afrikaans labourers are of their masters. "The poor white will make no effort because he feels the rich man is there only to take advantage of him."[45] When Pauline Smith was writing her short story she changed the emphasis. No class motive is given for Andries Lombard's twisted outlook and it is his illness which causes his perversity. Mintje's gentleness and dignity are suggested to the author by Doeri. "He (the miller) now called Doeri, and I was struck again by Doeri's beauty, or the remains of it, her skin so beautifully clear and her face so full of charm that one forgot her wretchedness and poverty and thought of her as somebody rather fine and wonderful."[46] In another part the reader is told "Up at the mill we saw Mr. Miller, his wife and several children, his wife a very beautiful woman still, with a clear, soft pale skin and a beautiful name 'Doertje' for Dorothea."[47]

Interestingly, Pauline Smith obtains the idea for the eelskin for which Mintje is said to have "tramped sixteen miles down the Aangenaam Valley to borrow from old Tan' Betje Ferreira"[48] from another source. When she was visiting the Mill River farm for the first time, Thys's wife related an incident. Pauline writes: "Mrs. Taute told us of Fred's throat and how they cured it of rheumatism by wrapping an eelskin round it."[49]

V   *"The Schoolmaster"*

The inspiration for this story arose mainly from a tale told to Pauline Smith by Thys Taute on her first visit to his farm. He was reminiscing about his upcountry treks. At one time he was a transport driver, carrying furniture, store goods, and bags of meal to the copper miners in O'Kiep in Namaqualand.

"And I'll tell you a queer thing P. There was a German up there who spent his life pushing a handcart across the desert, across Namaqualand and Kimberley. An old queer man he was and my father would not believe it when I told him, but it was true. It was a handcart like they used in stores. And he pushed it across the desert as a penance for putting out the eyes of his mules. He had a mulecart and did a sort of transport business with it, and one day the mules struck and in a rage he put out their eyes. And out of remorse for that he harnessed himself to a handcart and they said his breast was as hard as leather from the leather strap harnessing him to the cart. And it's queer but no harm ever came to him. For years he lived so. He would come to a village, and the store man and the policeman would take him food and things out to his cart, and he would stay there, outside the village, perhaps 2 or 3 days, and the next morning he would have disappeared, no one knew where. And everywhere in the kraals they fed him. *He was to them a sort of Evil Spirit,* they fed him and treated him kindly because they were afraid of him and wanted him to go on to the next kraal or village [italics mine]. And so he had always plenty to live on. He was of course queer in his head, but it was a wonderful life that he lived pushing his handcart across the desert and back again. And when he got to drifts he had a sort of pulley, and would fix the pulley in the ground and drag the handcart across on that."[50]

This extract illustrates how effectively Pauline Smith could transmute raw material and obtain richer and more concentrated effects. She transposes the story of the unknown German to the Little Karoo and causes an innocent young girl to fall in love with him. That characteristic of the German described clumsily by Thys ("He was to them a sort of Evil Spirit") is changed into the air of mystery surrounding Jan Boetje. The passing reference to the German's putting out the eyes of his mules is dramatically and horrifically enlarged.

One of the most arresting descriptions in this story comes from an entirely different source. Engela describes the view from the wagon-house which had been turned into a schoolroom. "From the door one looked out to the orange grove, where all my grandmother's children and many of her grandchildren also had been christened."[51] Pauline Smith records a custom of this kind during her second visit to Mimi Bergh at Kruis River East, when she had gone to visit Ouma Schoemann. She notes, "The orange grove is very beautiful, and the view from the wide grass paths across to the Swartberg Mountains very very fine and inspiring. It was in this grove that one of Mimi's brothers was christened. In the olden time the christening service was often held out of doors, and very beautiful it must have been, I think."[52]

VI *Miscellaneous*

Pauline Smith's humorous short story "The Cart" is likewise based solidly upon a story told to her while she was touring in South Africa. The narrator is again Thys Taute. Seldom did any character or incident outside the Little Karoo strike her imagination with sufficient force to cause her to incorporate it in her later work. An exception was an account given to her by an elderly lady whom she had known formerly as Mrs. Blake. This Mrs. Blake had come in her old age to marry a Mr. Morris. It is his story which provides the germ of an idea for her one-act play, "The Last Voyage." Mrs. Morris's words recorded in the journal show clearly what the theme of the play is:

"Yes and how strange it all worked out. 'I'm not hiding from you as it will be a difficult job being my father's wife,' Mrs. Titterton says to me, 'but you'll have a home and the gratitude of us all if you take the old man,' she says. 'We don't know how to make him comfortable. Six months he's here, and the children make a noise one day and he packs up and is off to England, and six months he's home again.' And it was like that too after I married him. Always backwards and forwards, and then the last time just coming out to die. You see some one had once said every voyage added 10 years to his life, and he was terribly afraid to die, and believed it, and it got to be a sort of craze with him. He was always adding 10 years to his life to cheat Death. Yes. He was afraid to die, he was. Just afraid."[53]

Not only do the long sequences and stories referred to here provide Pauline Smith with material for creative writing. There are many other episodes and observations in the journal which can be found reflected later in her work. Here follow a few random examples. On one occasion she was driven in a cart from George to Knysna by a Coloured driver, O'Villem, who was much cry and little wool, but jovial and appealing all the same. She writes: "Always before descending the passes to cross the rivers O'Villem wound his horn, playing long tunes on it, to appears to be the original for Jafta, the post-cart driver in *The Beadle*, who "would seize his bugle and warn all travellers on warn approaching carts and wagons of our coming."[54] He the straight grey and dusty road of the approach of his yellow body and red wheels."[55] The forked sticks she noticed next to the roads on some of the farms recur in her novel. "Jafta climbed out of the cart and hung a mailbag on a solitary post standing upright in the veld."[56] While visiting Ouma Schoemann with Mimi Bergh, Pauline noticed that she wore her housekeys on a chain at her side. These keys are given to Andrina in *The Beadle*. Her description of Mrs. Black at Faure suggests that she may have taken a hint for the character of Johanna Steenkamp. "She would be, I think, hard and intolerant in her judgement of others. The intolerance that is partly the result of a certain form of religion."[57]

The *South African Journal* is studded with observations and comments which have a close bearing on her writing. Not only are they of interest to a student of the origins of a work of fiction; they also illustrate the kind of writer that she was. She was not like the authors of Wild West stories or of love and science fiction, who present light entertainment and an escape from the real world either into impossible violence or into impossible sentiment. Her aim was to be as truthful as possible; in fact, it was to reflect reality by conveying it in a poetically heightened and concentrated form. Sometimes she falls short of the mark. Her imagination does not possess virtuosity; it is stirred by a limited number of themes and emotions. On occasions it is not sufficiently powerful to sustain an effect. But when she succeeds, hers is real writing—in the same territory where Tolstoy, Jane Austen, and Joseph Conrad practised. The great amount of source material in the journal serves to remind the reader that her creative work was intimately bound up with real life and living characters.

The journal is straightforward and commonsensical. An interesting instance of Pauline Smith's practicality occurs in the following episode. While she was visiting a Miss Wood in Cape Town she was introduced to an artist just out from England. This lady thought a great deal of herself and had a superior attitude towards the "colonials." Pauline writes:

And then in the same dignified and gentle tone of superiority she showed us a view from the Beach Hotel, Durban, "where we got such *beautiful* food," lifting the food somehow to a sort of heavenly standard with no comfortable physical connection whatever. I can't explain it but it gave me the impression that the lady would enjoy a good hearty meal not for the good of her body but simply for the good of her soul, and I don't know what the vegetarian (a Miss Metlerkamp, who was also visiting) felt about it but I felt the lady herself deceived herself and comfort meant as much to her as heaven or art![58]

There is nothing pretentious or superior in Pauline Smith's nature. She does not labour under any illusions about class or the burdens of the sensitive. The everyday tasks of life interest her as much as intellectual talk or literature. She would just as soon be listening to the stories of a Coloured kitchen maid as reading a book. The *South African Journal* provides ample proof for what the reader may have suspected from her novels and short stories alone; namely, that Pauline Smith has created literature because she was not "literary" and "highbrow" in ordinary life.

CHAPTER 10

A Suggestion of Eden

WHEN Pauline Smith wrote the children's sketches collected in *Platkops Children* she was re-creating for her own consolation an innocent and carefree life which seemed to her more perfect and joyful than that she was experiencing in her English exile. These sketches have the mystery and vividness of a child's vision. The rambling garden where Pato and Paoli played, the exciting circus and fairground characters, the secret, golden jackal which wandered near the walls at night, were all part of a more perfect and exciting world. In her imagination Platkops dorp (or Oudtshoorn) had been a kind of Garden of Eden.

This near-perfect environment is carried over into her later short stories and novel. Juriaan and Deltje van Royen live close to nature in the mountains above the Aangenaam Valley. Their lives are quiet and harmonious. Part of the Aangenaam Valley is the community of Harmonie, where Meneer and Mevrouw van der Merwe have learned to live in obedience to the will of God. The regular round of the seasons, the occasional thanksgiving services, and the rigorously ordered society all contribute to the impression of a sane and peaceful existence.

Not all the people who live here are innocent or at rest in their minds. Andries Lombard, Aalst Vlokman, Johanna Steenkamp, and Tan' Linda de Neysen are all in inner turmoil on account of past sins unforgiven, bitter selfrighteousness, or foolish ambitions. But when men or women are in accord with the spirit of the place, they can enjoy serenity. Such people are the van Royens, Alida van der Merwe, and young Andrina.

Unfortunately, some evil or temptation which threatens to overthrow the old ways enters into this world of quiet and simplicity. In the case of the van Royens it is the pain, the "mysterious and powerful third person who, for incomprehensible reasons, clutched at Deltje's side and forced her to lie helpless for hours on the low, wooden bedstead in the little bedroom."[1] For Andrina it is Henry Nind, the irresponsible and dallying Englishman who sees the Afrikaans girl as the plaything for a moment.

In *The Beadle* there is a garden next to the Harmonie farmhouse reminiscent of the garden in which the little girls of *Platkops Children* had played: a "tangled wilderness of roses, wistaria and plumbago in early bloom."[2] Around it is a stone wall, and through it runs a mountain stream. This stream makes an island of red rock in the centre of the garden where the young child, Jantje, often plays.

He loved just here to lie flat on his stomach and let the waters slip through his thin fingers like a living thing—to catch it, toss it, and see it fall, in showers of diamonds, to lie glistening on the red rock. Thoughout life the shadow of a great rock in a dry and thirsty land meant for Jantje the shadow of the rock in his grandmother's garden, and the River of Water of Life, the little brown stream that flowed round it.[3]

Seeing this garden through the eyes of the child helps the reader to understand it as a place of innocence, joy, and mystery. It is tangled, wild, and surrounded by a wall, like Eden. Here Andrina plays with the boy, sharing and understanding his imaginative and sensitive life. The importance of the garden as a symbol is strengthened by the fact that it occupies a central position in the four-part scheme of the novel. Andrina meets the Englishman often in the garden, and she is seduced in the small outside room which adjoins it.

This leads the reader to consider the role of Henry Nind. There is a hint that he is playing the role of a Satan. Bursting into the closed, simple community with his wider knowledge of the world, his "exhilaration of spirit which was almost triumph,"[4] and his desire to rebel, he is a free and potentially dangerous agent. From the outset of the novel his lawless and colourful qualities are stressed. The yellow and red post-cart in which he arrives, itself an intrusion into the slow, peaceful community, is a fitting vehicle for him. When this stupid, gay man sees the beauties of the spring he is moved, not to appreciation, but to "live his life as he pleased among these simple people and make of it what he would, regardless of his relatives in Princestown."[5]

Rebellion against order and acceptance is the most Satanic characteristic of Henry Nind. The serpent in the Eden story tempts Eve to eat what is forbidden, misleading her as to the results of her action and disguising his real motives. Similarly, the Englishman seduces Andrina, making her an outcast in her community and leading her up the garden path by hiding the fact that she is just a passing interest to him. Like Jan Boetje in *The Little Karoo* short stories, Henry Nind becomes a schoolmaster in the community. Both Andrina and Jantje are to learn English from him. He is installed in the outside room whose window overlooked the garden—this "wilderness full of strange and beautiful and unexpected things watered by the stream from the mill."[6]

Soon it becomes apparent that Nind is a teacher in a wider sense, bringing experience, and bitter experience, to Andrina. In his schoolroom he hints that with the aid of his dictionary there was much more he could teach her—"much that he was anxious and impatient to teach her—if she were but willing to learn. Was she willing?"[7] Andrina's heart beats wildly as she grows aware of his earnestness:

The Englishman, she knew, was not referring to "school" as she understood it, but anything that he desired to teach her she was willing to learn . . . Her mind, her heart, her soul—all these were now his and he might do what he would with them.[8]

In "The Schoolmaster" Engela had learned the joy and sadness of love from Jan Boetje. Andrina also is to understand the temptations of jealousy and the misery of loneliness after the Englishman decides to go away.

The reader must be on his guard against drawing too close a parallel with the Eden story. If Jan Boetje and Henry Nind have Satanic qualities, it is as true to say that they develop and deepen the experience of the two young women. Both are men, and are greatly loved—the Adams to these Eves. Pauline Smith's primary interest is in men and women as she saw them around her, the living, imperfect people. Consequently, there can never be more than a suggestion of the Eden tale which can have taken place only in a world which no longer exists and lies more properly in the realm of the theologian. Pauline Smith's concern for everyday life shows her that imperfection is universal and that it has to be accepted and lived with. "And if I let none that have sinned travel in my wagon who then would travel in it, Andrintje?"[9] asks Hans Rademeyer, the old and gentle transport rider in *The Beadle*. People who refuse to acknowledge their own weakness are often the worse for it. As Aalst Vlokman realised, righteousness could prove "a terrible weapon for evil."[10]

Andrina grows in stature and dignity of character after she has been seduced and has learned to accept her sorrows. Engela has grown from childhood to womanhood with her tragic, unfulfilled love for Jan Boetje. Juriaan and Deltje van Royen are braver and more admirable as they return from the hospital in Platkops dorp to their home in the mountains, knowing that Deltje's pain will not be cured, yet accepting it and what life remains to her.

Pauline Smith always puts humanity first. God is of interest to her only in the way that He appears in the faith, thoughts, and fears of men and women. She sees so much dignity in the suffering of men and women and so much mystery in ultimate death, that the lives of ordinary, mortal people seem superior even to the eternal existence of the resurrected Christ as we read of it in the New Testament. In *The Beadle* the Pastor has been talking to Andrina about the love of God—the way in which He sent His Son as a sacrifice for men's sins. After Niklaas Joosten has gone, she thinks about his words.

She tried to grasp the full meaning of the sacrifice made for her by the Son of God . . . but what was this sacrifice of which the pastor spoke with tears in his eyes? Did the Son of God not know Himself to be the Son of God? Did He not know that He would rise again and go to His Father? Out of all eternity where lay the sacrifice, in time, of a life on earth of thirty years? What sacrifice could there be for one who *knew* that death was to end in so triumphant a resurrection? . . . If Christ had been but the son of Joseph, not of God, if He had died not to rise again, but to lie for ever in the grave, then, thought Andrina, she could have understood and loved Him.[11]

Generally it is dangerous to attribute the thoughts of a character in a work of fiction to the author. But in this case passages from the *South African Journal*[12] show that these speculations of Andrina accord well with Pauline Smith's own religious opinions. Moreover, this is an occasion on which the simple, unintellectual farm girl falls out of character by bothering herself with subtle and relatively complex ideas; and this further suggests that it is the creator and not the creation speaking.

God's love of righteousness and hate of sin do not force themselves upon the attention of those whose gaze is focused on men and women in their everyday lives. Rather, sins are seen to enlarge a person's experience and to heighten his dignity when he suffers under and learns to live with his own faults. This viewpoint can be found in Pauline Smith, even though she realises from observation that wrongdoing brings its inevitable consequences. If she had been a theologian, she would have condemned sin because of her concern with God and his promise that he would punish it. As an artist, she describes sin in action, showing its aftermath, but accepting and valuing it as one of the characteristics of human nature.

All this implies that the Eden story can have only a limited value for her. The *South African Journal* showed how she had a difference of opinion with Miss Julia Morris about it. After that friendly argument she wrote:

It is no good explaining to her that the story of Adam and Eve is quite as true for me in a way as it is literally for her. She thinks I am only the "most frivolous person" she has ever met![13]

The garden of Paradise is true for Pauline Smith in its hold upon her imagination. The poetic force of the story makes itself felt in her work—the simple gardens, the order and disorder symbolism, the serene cycle of the seasons, and the motif of temptation. But by their very nature these things cannot be captured in schemes or definitions. They constitute the evocative but elusive suggestion of Eden.

CHAPTER 11

Pauline Smith and Afrikaans

IN Pauline Smith's novel and short stories there is a good picture not only of the people of the Little Karoo and their community life, but also of the way they frame their words and the mannerisms of their speech. Although Oudtshoorn had a small number of English-speaking people when she spent her childhood there, the surrounding farms were run almost entirely by Afrikaners whose only language was Afrikaans.

Afrikaans, or Dutch, as Pauline Smith calls it, has come to great prominence in South Africa. Nowadays it is not only an official language but is beginning to own a considerable literature, especially in the field of poetry. Although it bears some resemblance to High Dutch, from which it sprang, it is quite independent with a flavour and rhythm of its own. Its development can be traced back for many generations. It is the language developed by the descendants of the Dutch free-burghers who came early to live in South Africa. Working their own farms, with interests which were different if not counter to those of the Dutch East India Company officials, it was not long before they were cut off from their native Holland in fact and in spirit.

Subjected to new climates and terrain, influenced by the new, strange indigenous people and, to a slight extent by the slaves from the Far East, Afrikaners introduced new methods of cooking and running their houses. What is more, they began to speak in a new way. As early as the end of the eighteenth century a satirical song, *"Lied ter ere van de Swellendamsche en diverse andere helden bij die bloedige actie aan Muisenberg in dato 7 Aug. 1795"* ["Song in honour of the Swellendam and various other heroes in the bloody action at Muizenberg, on 7th August, 1795"], shows that Afrikaans differs considerably from the Dutch.

This song, written to poke fun at the commando of free-burgher volunteers from Graaff-Reinet and Swellendam who virtually ran away from the British after a short engagement, features its Afrikaans in the mimicked language of the men from Swellendam and "other heroes."

As the Afrikaners gradually became aware of their identity as a people, their pride in their language grew. In the late nineteenth century a language movement was initiated, and more and more writers began to appear. The South African War brought literature and the organised development of language to a halt. After this period of disruption, however, Afrikaans seemed to surge forward with renewed vigour, rather like a river which gains energy from being dammed up behind a temporary obstruction. The second language movement was on a larger scale than the first. Dictionaries were commenced; spelling began to be standardised; Afrikaans was a language on its own.

In Pauline Smith's dialogue there are echoes of Afrikaans rhythms and syntax. Indeed, recognising how successfully she has rendered the feel of the Afrikaans spoken word into English can be one of the greatest delights to a reader who knows something of that language. One South African critic, Mr. Charles Eglington, feels she has done this so successfully and compellingly that he writes:

I have not been able to discover how well Pauline Smith actually knew Afrikaans—the Afrikaans spoken by simple, remote and isolated country people towards the end of the last century; but it is abundantly apparent that she understood them perfectly, had a particularly sensitive ear for the cadences of their speech, and their manner of expressing themselves, and that she was very alive to the idiosyncratic nuances of speech, which reveal, rather than conceal, character.[1]

Biographical facts remove any doubt and show that Pauline Smith did not know Afrikaans well. Miss Marie Stegmann, her old friend in Oudtshoorn, told me that, although she could understand a little of Afrikaans conversations, she could not speak the language. In this she was following in the footsteps of her father, Dr. Smith, whose prolonged dealings with the farming families in the district of Oudtshoorn never seem to have induced him to learn their language. Apparently most of his

Pauline Smith and Afrikaans

instructions were given in a frenzied, complicated, and occasionally comical sign language with a few words of English or Dutch thrown in for good measure!

In her *South African Journal* Pauline Smith refers to her poor understanding of Afrikaans when she records a visit to a woman in Mossel Bay. She was received by a Coloured servant. The girl settled her down with some books; and then followed what she calls "a pleasant short conversation in Dutch of which I understood nothing."[2] On another occasion she is driving out in the veld looking at the flowers and plants. She tries to describe what she sees in terms of English species, and O' Villem, the Hottentot driver, keeps on telling her the local Afrikaans names. She writes: "He told us lots of names, but goodness knows how to spell them."[3] Had she been at all familiar with Afrikaans she would have had no difficulty in jotting down a few simple names.

Perhaps we can gauge her grasp of Afrikaans most accurately in two letters to her friend, Miss Ethel Campbell, in which she humorously tries to write in that language. These letters show that her vocabulary was small and her spelling hazardous. For readers who have some knowledge of Afrikaans one letter and an extract from another are reproduced below. Notice that whenever a word eludes her, or the thought grows too complicated, she breaks into English.

Maritzburg.

My liewe Ethel,
Ek sal vir jou in jou soorte Afrikaans sckrief as ek lê op my kooi in de huis van de vrou van de Burgomeister. Ek het baai baai jammer geword om jou te laat staan op die straat gister en vir mij hier te kom alles alles aleen—Jij het mij baaie baaie (groetness) en goetness gedoen, en ik kan vir jou niets sê ni maar Dankie en Dankie want jy sê alle die tyd-"Ach pouf!" as ik ander worde praat—Ek het nie my lees book hier nie en ek het nie my Dictionarie. So jy moet my spelling en grammar en alles eskuis—Dankie!
Ek het an jou baaie baaie gedenk in die naant van die ratte hartloop in die solder boont mij kop! Ek sal never? so in friendin vir krij (krey?) dat sal vir mij so baaie dinkies doen as jy sal vir mij doen all die tyd dat ek het met jou en jou moede en jou broer gewoon—
Jy is n' goede goede vriendin en ek hou van jou baaie baaie en Eskuis! Dankie![4]

She sends a second note to Ethel Campbell from Oudtshoorn:

My dear Ethel—Nie mij liewe E!
Ek was so blij om joue letter te krij, mar mij Afrikaans is nou baie
sleg! Jy sccrif baie better as mij—ek scrif as I spell—altogether badly
sitting in my (room?) on a day of cold pelting rain with snow on
the Swartberg mountains! Most unusual for this time of the year.[5]

In English the letters would run roughly as follows:

My dear Ethel,
I shall write to you in your kind of Afrikaans as I lie on my bed
in the house of the Mayor's wife. I was very very sorry to leave you
standing on the street yesterday and for you to come and fetch me
here quite by yourself. You did me a great deal of kindness, and I
can say nothing to you but Thank You and Thank You, because you
always say "Oh pouff!" if I say anything else. I don't have my reading book here, and I don't have my dictionary. So you will have to
excuse my spelling and grammar and everything—Thank you!
I thought about you a great deal in the night when the rats ran
in the ceiling right on top of my head! I shall never find such a friend
who will do so many little things for me as you did all the time that
I was staying with your mother, your brother and yourself—
You are a good, good friend and I am very very fond of you.
Excuse me! Thank you!

And:

My dear Ethel—No, my dear E!
I was so happy to get your letter, but now my Afrikaans is very
bad! You write much better than I do—I write as I spell—altogether
badly. . . .

Indeed, Pauline Smith needed her reading book and her dictionary as she herself well knew! The English translations have
hidden much of the clumsiness in the original letters. She uses
grammatical constructions which would be idiomatic in English
but are naïve in Afrikaans. Her spelling is conjectural to say the
least! And when she does not know an Afrikaans word she pops
in an English one, sometimes well disguised: for example, "Dictionarie," "ratte," and "better." It is unlikely that she could have

had any intellectual understanding of subtle nuances in Afrikaans speech.

How, then, could Pauline Smith give so forceful an impression of Afrikaans in her English dialogue when she had no perfect knowledge of the language? The answer to this lies in her recognition that there were great similarities between the Little Karoo and its people and the world of the Old Testament. In *A.B.* . . . *'a minor marginal note'* she writes:

Such taste and feeling as I had for English letters had come not from intelligence, but from the deep impression made upon me in my South African childhood by the beauty and simplicity of the Old Testament stories (whose country and people were so like my own).[6]

Moreover, she found early that the "slow and brooding talk"[7] of the Afrikaans farmers and *bywoners* "fell so naturally in translation into the English of the Old Testament."[8] This realisation has guided her in her writing of dialogue. Occasionally she introduces literal translations of more obvious Afrikaans expressions into her speech. But generally speaking the Old Testament parallel is the key to her success.

It is interesting to see that when Pauline Smith is aiming at light or comical dialogue, literally translated expressions, or "Afrikanerisms," are most prominent. A good example can be taken from *The Beadle* when the fumbling and down-to-earth suitor to Andrina, Jan Beyers, asks Tan' Linda de Neysen to press on with the courtship on his behalf. Contrary to all expectations, Andrina has turned down his offer of marriage which had been made by letter (a tradition in the Aangenaam Valley). But Aalst Vlokman has offered Beyers two plough-oxen with her, and he is determined not to take no for an answer. In this scene both the yokel, Beyers, and Tan' Linda are excited. Their language is stretched to the utmost of its simple eloquence and clumsy satire.

"*Now look, now*, Jan Beyers," said Tan' Linda firmly, "if Andrina has said that she will not have your letter it is *now* finished! Can a man take a wife against her will?"

"*No, what!*" persisted the young man obstinately, "but surely if you and the beadle speak for me Andrina will take my letter!"

"The beadle!" cried Tan' Linda in amazement. "The beadle? And what then has the beadle to do with Andrina's letter?" . . .

"I met *now* the beadle in the river bed this morning, and he *spoke with me* about Andrina du Toit," he said at last.

"And what did he say, Jan Beyers?"

"*No, what*, Juffrouw," said the young man unhappily, plunging to his doom, "he said that to the man that married Andrina there would go the two plough-oxen from his lands." . . .

"Tell me, now," she cried, wagging an accusing finger at him, "tell me, now! Is it Andrina or the two plough-oxen that have run three hours through your mind?"

"*No, what*, Juffrouw," protested the young man foolishly, "*no, what!*"⁹

The humour in this passage springs from the old woman's fussy questions, her curiosity, and Jan Beyers's oafish attempts to deny the truth. Pauline Smith gains much of her comical effect by including Afrikaans expressions which give the English a new, odd rhythm. All the words and phrases given in italics seem to owe their existence in the dialogue to Afrikaans. Tan' Linda's "Now look, now" echoes the Afrikaans expression "*Kyk nou!*" Jan Beyers's clumsy reiteration of "no, what" seems a direct translation of the expression "*nee wat.*" The intrusive "now" in "I met now the beadle" is designed to suggest a construction in Afrikaans. Finally, "he spoke with me" seems a reproduction of "*hy het met my gepraat.*"

When Pauline Smith is writing dialogue with more serious or elevated content, she tends either to cut down on the number of literally translated phrases from Afrikaans or to eliminate them. An example occurs just after Aalst Vlokman has walked down to the Harmonie church to be in time for the thanksgiving service. The beadle's mind is burdened with guilt and misery. He feels himself responsible for Jacoba's death, and he is worried about what might be happening to Andrina. As he approaches the Church, he hears the Pastor speaking to the people.

"My little children, speak no evil of the living if you would praise the dead. To judge is not for us. Seek each of you forgiveness for his own sin, grant each of you forgiveness for the sins of others—God

Himself has commanded it. Is there one of us that is without sin? Let him that would listen to the evil that is spoken of another acknowledge first the evil that is within himself, and who then will dare to listen? Who then will dare to speak?"[10]

Pauline Smith has not tried in any obvious way to show that these words are in Afrikaans. The phrasing, the general ring of the address, even the selection of individual words such as *seek* and *grant*, show that this dialogue is patterned on Biblical English. Yet it does not appear antiquated or out of place. The language conveys the character of the Pastor and the spirit of the service perfectly. In other more serious passages Pauline Smith combined Biblical language with occasional translated Afrikaans expressions to great effect. After Aalst Vlokman has listened to the words of the Pastor, he is moved to confess his past and his relationship with Andrina before the whole congregation.

"Mijnheer! If they would judge Andrina let them first judge me! If evil be spoken of her let it first be spoken of me. What is Andrina's sin to mine? It is not for Andrina's shame that Jacoba lies now in her grave. It is for mine. I that was to have married Jacoba took from her sister Klaartje that which she would not give me and Klaartje's child is mine. Afterwards, when Herman du Toit found how it was with her, he left her. Klaartje died for my sin when our child was born. And Jacoba died the day that I would not stay in the orchard to read Andrina's letter with her but asked her what was Klaartje's child to me."[11]

These words, spoken at a moment of high emotion, have strong Biblical rhythms. Such a sentence as "If evil be spoken of her, let it first be spoken of me" is clearly inspired in cadence and construction by the Old Testament. On the other hand the unusually placed "now," certain peculiarities of syntax, and the expression "how it was with her" are echoes of Afrikaans.

Mr. Eglington notes that "Pauline Smith's Afrikaans-into-English dialogue leaves an echo in the mind—an echo which tends to condition the memory of readers, and leave them with the impression that the diction in the dialogue is to some extent characteristic of her prose in general."[12] This is very true. Any passage of straight description, such as the opening of *The Beadle* or the story of Alie van Staden's trek in "Desolation," is in perfect standard English. The dialogue tends to impart its flavour to the whole of the writing, giving the impression of a unique and unusual style.

However, it is important to remember that the success of her dialogue is due not only to her understanding that the language of her characters could be rendered into English through the diction of the Old and New Testaments. Biblical influence is apparent in every part of her creative effort. Her symbolism, the faith and natures of her men and women, are conceived also in Biblical terms. They combine with the spoken words to form a single and convincing picture of life. The dialogue is only one aspect of the total picture. It is, as Mr. Eglington suggests, "a language that has been transfused from reality, created by a remarkable imagination."[13]

CHAPTER 12

The Poetry Behind the Facts

IT IS APPARENT that Pauline Smith wishes her reader to be
moved in a special way by places like the Aangenaam Valley,
the Credo Mountains and the farm Harmonie. He is expected to
feel through them her intuition of a remote and perfect region.
They are, as has been made clear, suggestions of Eden. This
talent of hers to invest ordinary objects and situations with
poetic strength gives power to her work.

The high land where the van Royens live above the Aangenaam
Valley is a place to be close to spiritual reality. The cold, square
hospital on the banks of the river in Platkops dorp, standing in
its open yard, is symbolic of the brashness and lack of compassion in the practical medicine which it subserves. Many other
descriptions and situations point to specific meanings which are
suggested by but lie beyond themselves. These save the stories
from becoming colonial sketches of interest primarily for their
local colour.

Even the cycle of the seasons is invested with a certain
poetical meaningfulness in stories like "The Miller" and "The
Schoolmaster," and especially in *The Beadle.* Its symbolism seems
to state that when a man accepts and conforms to the seasons
he has interior peace. Sin and bitter self-righteousness throw
him out of gear with the round of nature. This is true of Andries
Lombard who refuses to plant his lands in spring and digs a
grave when his neighbours are bringing in the harvest. Only at
the moment of his death does he become one with the year, by
bringing his repentance as "fruit" to the thank-offering service.

The Beadle's strong seasonal pattern gives the book shape and
plays an important part in the development of the characters of
Aalst Vlokman and Andrina. The book is divided into four parts.

The first of these plays itself out in early spring. When Henry Nind comes into the Aangenaam Valley he sees that "the corn was already up and the fresh young green of mealies was showing through the dark grey soil. The little orchards were pink with peach blossom and the veld too, grey and bare for so many months of each year, was gay with spring flowers."[1]

With the spring there is a general stirring in the Harmonie community. Harry feels lawless and exultant. It is a special year for Andrina who, ever the child of nature, is growing into womanhood with the awakening season. At this time her aunts set about making her sacrament dress, suggestive of her womanhood, and Jacoba gives her a mirror, one of the tokens of self-awareness which occur frequently in Pauline Smith's work. This spring also makes demands on Aalst Vlokman. But, like Andries Lombard, his bitterness and past sin make him go against it. He hates to think that Andrina is growing up, and is lonely and sullen.

The second part covers only a short period of time, the weeks of "high spring." Action is centered mainly in Mevrouw van der Merwe's garden. At this time, when blood is hot, Henry Nind and Andrina are attracted strongly to each other. The sacrament dress is completed, and the church service ratifies that she has now reached womanhood by admitting her to the adult congregation. In this part Aalst Vlokman receives his greatest blows. His offer to the Lord of two plough-oxen to save Andrina is rejected. Johanna gains the mastery of him and his whole attempt at guarding his illegitimate daughter seems to be in ruins. For him it is a period of bitterness and disillusion.

In part three "the clear spring days grew warmer with the approaching heat of summer."[2] It is in early summer that Andrina and Harry become lovers—the heated blood and rising emotions of the spring have reached their fruition. Throughout the summer Andrina has "a life of dear and secret intimacy with the Englishman."[3] All this while Aalst Vlokman is dazed and unhappy. Life is empty and dark for him. He is in complete opposition to the summer. Autumn and the fall of the year come on with the end of this section. Harry, who in his own opinion has philandered long enough, decides to go away. Andrina, always in harmony with her surroundings, experiences sorrow and emptiness after his departure at the same time as the onset of winter.

The fourth part has for its time span autumn and winter, concluding with the re-arrival of spring. Thus it brings the book round full circle in a pleasing and appropriate manner. In autumn Aalst Vlokman slowly begins to show the fruits of regeneration. By early winter, the time of the thanksgiving service, his repentance and resignation are ripe. Down at the church, in front of all the congregation, he confesses that he is Andrina's father and takes the responsibility for Jacoba's death upon his own shoulders. Although he does not realise it, he is now conforming to the spirit of the thanksgiving service. He has to leave Harmonie and all which is dear to him, once more plunging into isolation. But this time he has a purpose—to find out where his daughter is and to offer to work for her. His personal winter is now in harmony with the season. It is a healthy state, the period of sapless wood which must precede the new bud.

During this winter Andrina is compelled to leave her home. She is assailed by desolation and despair after Harry has left and is tempted to be jealous of Lettice Featherstone. With the knowledge that she is bearing a child, she leaves Uitkijk and throws herself upon the protection of old Hans Rademeyer, who takes her to the toll-house in the Cortes district where his sister lives. Both father and daughter have to leave their old ways of life and journey in uncertainty and solitude before they can meet with new love and understanding in the next spring. Aalst Vlokman is no longer bitter and against the seasons; he accepts the re-awakening year with a certain simple wonder and happiness. When Andrina is lying in the toll-house room waiting for her father to enter, she thinks: "At Harmonie now, in the orchard there, the peach trees were surely in blossom."[4] But this spring there is a new child, "the little grandson . . . with his round bald head."[5] Aalst Vlokman who was filled with bitterness and resentment as his child became a woman, can now accept the infant and ask if he may work for it.

As Mr. William Plomer suggests in his preface to *The Little Karoo*[6] the symbolic situation of Anna Coetzee cranking at the handle of her broken musical box may be a trifle emphatic. However, other situations and objects have a poetic strength which is both luminous and intriguing. Their more compelling hold derives, perhaps, from the fact that their meanings are not as obvious.

One of the more important of these symbolic objects is a mirror in a frame of shells. It is mentioned three times in *The Little Karoo* and *The Beadle*. First it is part of a small box and one of Deltje van Royen's treasured possessions in "The Pain." As she travels across the wide, desolate veld in her husband's trek-cart, racked with pain and afraid on her momentous journey to the Platkops dorp hospital, she keeps it close to her, almost —as Mr. Plomer suggests—like a talisman. What can this small seemingly worthless object mean to her? Is it some consolation, a reminder of a happier past? Or does it represent self-awareness?

It takes another short story, "The Sinner," to give the mirror a more definite symbolic meaning. Here it is owned by Jacoba Nooi, the silly woman with a tongue like a running sluice, who persuades Niklaas Dampers to abandon his wife, life, and family to rush madly into the Kombuis. The mirror was such as "had never before been seen by any bijwoner's wife or daughter in the Platkops district."[7] It represents a new dimension in self-awareness and is a potential temptation to pride and vanity. Niklaas's wife and neighbours realise this, but he has been so wrapped up in himself that Jacoba catches him unawares. When he sits with her on the river bank and she suddenly brings her mirror into play, "Niklaas saw before him part of his own wild and sorrowful face, and part of Koba Nooi's plump, round, childish one pressing against it."[8]

Apart from the old cracked glass at which he had glanced when dressing for church, the *bywoner* had never used a mirror before. Now he was seeing his own image, languorously and with intense self-awareness, for the first time. He sees the outward manifestations of his inner state and finds himself imperfect and disordered. At once he gives himself up in a frenzied despair and tries to forget everything in making love with Jacoba Nooi. Although the mirror itself always remains the same, its effect differs, depending on the kind of person who looks into it. For Deltje van Royen the looking-glass could never be dangerous.

She can see herself without getting unbalanced from pride or fear. It is only people who are not one with themselves who are put off their stroke by the mirror.

The looking-glass with its frame of shells appears a third time in *The Beadle*. And here it has both of these effects. Jacoba Steenkamp, the humble, innocent sister of the self-righteous Johanna, buys the mirror for Andrina. The aunt is happy on account of the young woman's beauty and no doubt wants her niece to see herself and keep herself in trim. There is no pride here, harmless vanity at the most. Wonder and mystery are the greatest meanings the mirror has for her. In the scene where Jacoba hands it over to Andrina these qualities are stressed. They are near some graves—mysterious, unchanging death beside them—and the time is dusk.

Together, with beating hearts, they peered at themselves in the little square of glass through the fading light. . . . Andrina asked for no explanation of this miraculous gift, and Jacoba offered none.[9]

Aalst Vlokman, like Niklaas Dampers, is filled with harsh self-righteousness. He sees the mirror only as dangerous pride. When he thinks bitterly how his daughter may be seduced by Henry Nind, his mind moves to the mirror: "Jacoba, poor fool, might God forgive her! had given the child a mirror in which to learn her beauty."[10] But Andrina is simple and unself-conscious enough to escape this pitfall.

Of her gifts Andrina herself remained as unaware as she was of any God but Jehovah. In the little mirror rimmed with shells she had seen no beauty that was worthy of the Englishman's regard.[11]

Aalst Vlokman has no doubt been afraid of what the mirror will do to Andrina, because he cannot face his own image. Upright and fiercely competitive, Johanna realises this immediately after she has challenged the beadle to declare what his right to Andrina is. On an impulse she brings the mirror into the room.

"Look now, Aalst Vlokman," she said, propping it up against a dish on the table before him, "look well now into Jacoba's present,

for there you will see the face of the man that took Klaartje to
Platkops dorp and yet thinks he can say what Andrina shall wear
and whom she shall marry!"[12]

Like Niklaas Dampers, Aalst Vlokman sees in his own image
the outward sign of his restless and inconsistent spirit. Proud and
striving for perfection, he cannot face up to what he sees—"a man
abandoned by his God"[13]—and rises hurriedly to leave the room.
As he goes, the mirror slips from the table and breaks at the
leg of his stool. This scene suggests that he cannot face himself
or others in his present state. Willy-nilly, he must break and
change before he can escape from his own remorse and misery.

Another striking symbol in *The Beadle* is Andrina's sacrament
dress. It has been shown how the girl's acceptance into the
church was a sign of her achieved womanhood. The dress which
the two aunts make for her indicates to all the world that she is
a child no longer. It is made from a print material which "had
a pale grey ground, closely sprinkled with pin-prick black dots
over which were scattered small pink roses and little blue forget-
me-nots."[14] Tan' Jacoba, we are told, was thrilled with the
flowers. For her they suggested the beauty, delicacy, and fruit-
fulness of life and of Andrina's growing up. Tan' Johanna took a
grim comfort from the frequency of the little black dots. Andrina's maturity will bring austerity and disappointment as well
as joy. In this way the dress becomes a symbol for the whole of
Andrina's new life.

At first Aalst Vlokman is antagonistic both to this new,
attractive young woman and to her dress. With bitter pangs of
fear and inward protest he sees her in her new glory at the
church service. The dress becomes associated in his mind with
her sexual maturity and her chance of being seduced by Henry
Nind. He reproaches the Steenkamp sisters bitterly for dressing
her up like a doll for the Englishman to play with. Yet it is the
same dress which helps him to find Andrina at the end of the
novel. Alone and without obsessions, after confessing his sin at
Harmonie, the beadle is walking along the Cortes-dorp-Losberg
road. Suddenly he sees Andrina's sacrament dress hanging out
on a bush to dry. For the first time he can see the dress in its
beauty:

Those little pink roses—those little blue flowers on their background of grey, closely sprinkled with pin-prick black dots—anywhere on earth would the beadle have known them.[15]

The way in which he goes up to the bush and touches the dress reminds us of Tan' Jacoba's simple wonder at the colour of the material. As a symbol, the dress has remained the same. It still speaks of Andrina's new maturity. But Aalst Vlokman has changed. His acceptance has made him one with the seasons and put him in harmony with his whole world. Consequently the sacrament dress, which once had driven him nearly to distraction, has become an ally, showing him the way back to his daughter. It is "a sign from the Lord."[16]

The two plough-oxen which Aalst Vlokman offers to Jan Beyers if he will marry Andrina have symbolic significance in giving a picture of the beadle's spiritual state at that time. By sacrificing the beasts, he is trying to make a bargain with God. This is the Old Testament conception of justice: I give you this and you give me that—an eye for an eye and a tooth for a tooth. Appropriately, the oxen are typical sacrifice animals. Pauline Smith shows that this desire to bargain with God and human nature is inadequate and ridiculous. Her method of doing this is through a comic episode in which Jan Beyers tries to press his suit to Andrina. Whenever Andrina moved away from him, it seemed to Jan Beyers as if "the two plough-oxen were retreating with her."[17] It is not until the beadle's pride is broken that he understands the inadequacy of this type of justice and reaches the understanding of Mevrouw Alida van der Merwe that "sin would pass, sorrow would pass, but the compassion which had sent the Redeemer into the world to forgive and heal—this would never pass."[18]

He confesses his past and trudges away from the Harmonie community, a wanderer with no possessions save the bag upon his back. In this he ceases to be the Old Testament man, offering his goods as the pledge of a bargain with God. His new role is reminiscent of the disciples whom Christ sent by twos to announce the arrival of the new Kingdom.

Many other parts of Pauline Smith's writing are rich in poetic suggestion. The grave which Maqwasi digs for Ludovitje in the clay-stone *koppie,* the trees, the furrows, and the jailhouse which old Alie van Staden thinks of before she sets out on her long and desolate trek, are amongst them. Even the Southeaster in that rather thin one-act play, "The Last Voyage," is effectively symbolic when we come to realise that it represents the attrition of old age against which John Tunstall has fought so long. This poetry behind the facts is one of the most important characteristics of Pauline Smith's writing. Its effectiveness and prevalence form one of her strongest claims to excellence.

CHAPTER 13

A Strange, Austere and Tender Talent

ARNOLD Bennett, Pauline Smith's literary "master" and friend, seems to have pinpointed some of the best qualities of her writing in his introduction to *The Little Karoo*. Here he writes of himself as "perhaps the earliest wondering admirer of her strange, austere, tender, and ruthless talent."[1] Her work is indeed austere and the characterisation at times ruthlessly truthful. The style is economical and direct. No foibles or hidden weaknesses in her men and women escape her gaze.

A likeable woman like Jacoba Steenkamp in *The Beadle* is shown to possess weaknesses; and Johanna, who made a sin of self-righteousness and ruined her sisters' lives, has a certain grim, admirable courage and other good points. With patience and restraint Pauline Smith records a good quality in a character. With equal patience and restraint she notes a weakness. Although the reader is made to see that it is necessary for men like Niklaas Dampers and Aalst Vlokman to come to terms with themselves, he is in no way led to dislike or despise them. Pauline Smith does not play on his prejudices; she lets the facts speak for themselves. This impartiality is one of her greatest strengths. She faces up to reality at all times. Despite the yearning for a perfect state of life which pervades much of the description, her work is not escapist. Pain and inevitable death break in on the serene lives of the van Royens. Poverty and hardship are the lot of Alie van Staden. Drought and cancer, sexual frustration, and senseless accidents enter into Pauline Smith's world.

She is truthful also in her recognition that a man's actions and transgressions have their inevitable consequences. "Judge not that you be not judged. For with what judgment ye judge ye shall be judged: and with what measure ye mete, it shall be measured to you again"[2] is a saying which her observation has supported and exemplified in the lives of several of her characters. Andries Lombard realises just before his death that God had judged him only as long as he had proudly rejected his family and the rest of the community. Niklaas Dampers feels that God ceases to judge him as soon as he implores mercy and is no longer aggrieved at the sinfulness of others. Aalst Vlokman also escapes from a sensation of oppression when he confesses his sin and learns to accept. Sometimes, however, there is no escape from pride and judgment. Johanna Steenkamp's self-righteousness leads her to a solitude which even the love of Mevrouw Alida van der Merwe cannot penetrate. Piet Pienaar, the jealous father, loses all contact with reality, and he dies without being reconciled to or understanding his wife and son.

It is part of Pauline Smith's austerity and truthfulness to realise that, although a man's past sins may be forgiven, they can never be eradicated. Some time later they may confront him again, and he cannot pretend that he is innocent of them. The rich farmer, Meneer van Reenen, must realise that his wild youth in the Kombuis robs him of the right to condemn Niklaas Dampers for running off with Koba Nooi. When Burgert de Jager says that he will close his irrigation ditch and no longer exercise the water-rights for which he had fought so bitterly with Jan Redlinghuis, his daughter thinks that "the blood is already so deep in the lands that nothing we can do will now wash it out."[3]

Pauline Smith's truthfulness led her to include these harsh and sometimes depressing facts about human nature in her writing. It also enabled her to see the dignity and spiritual worth of the country Afrikaners at a time when it was the fashion amongst many English-speaking South Africans to think of them as backward and stupid. Her absolute freedom from group prejudice springs from her integrity and courage to have an individual approach.

Together with her austerity and truthfulness is a moving tenderness. She does not analyse her characters in order merely to expose their weaknesses or to assert their limitations triumphantly. It is because she values them that she is moved to portray them as they are. And she feels that she cannot establish their true stature unless every detail is noted down. She is not like a soulless anatomist, slitting skin and sinew to display the inward parts, but like the grand, humanistic scientists, still possessing a capacity for wonder, who anxiously record each detail of a plant or animal because they feel that something of the mysterious and precious detail of the world will otherwise be lost.

Tenderness and compassion are to her the greatest of human qualities. She realises that men and women cannot understand the amazingly complex justice of God, and any ideas they may have on the subject would be only poor approximations to the real thing. Consequently, the best thing a man can do is to accept others and to refrain altogether from judging them. Only then can he become great as a human being. This state is exemplified by Hans Rademeyer, Juriaan and Deltje van Royen, and Alie van Staden. Two other well-drawn characters, Andries Lombard and Aalst Vlokman, grow in stature as they win through to acceptance and love after bitter trial.

Arnold Bennett writes also of Pauline Smith's "strange" talent. To people in England the remote and often austere setting of the Little Karoo must have seemed unusual. More important, however, are the brooding faith and stark intensities of her characters. It has been seen that a suggestion of a more perfect world can be found in some of the settings and that the poetic energy of certain characters hints that they may be Satans or Tempters. At times her characters' emotions are screwed almost to the breaking point. Extreme frustration, demoniac jealousy, madness, and near madness all interest her. In "Ludovitje" and parts of "The Pain" the faith of her characters is so intense and moving that it approaches a kind of ecstatic mysticism reminiscent of the writing of John Bunyan. All these things taken together surely give her work an unusual and distinctive stamp.

It is odd that Pauline Smith should have been so fired by the simple, believing people whom for the most part she chooses for her characters, when she had doubts about the existence of God. Moreover, she showed herself to dislike organised religion —as the Anglican church—yet these men and women were all faithful members of the rigorous Dutch Reformed Church. God was of interest to her primarily as he showed himself in the lives of her characters. Nonetheless, that does not explain why these simple and faithful people should have inspired her rather than sophisticated and agnostic characters who, one might imagine, would have had more in common with her theories. It is an intriguing fact that, although she tends to be agnostic in religion and liberal and humanistic in her political thought, the energy of her imagination goes into re-creating a conservative, unchanging society whose main characteristics are a strong faith and an acceptance of a traditional social hierarchy.

The *South African Journal* illustrates that there is a close relation between what Pauline Smith saw and heard in her own life and what she includes in her short stories and novel. Moreover, some of her characters take substance from what she has felt herself. In *A.B. . . . 'a minor marginal note'* she confesses to this method of writing. "I could set down nothing which I did not 'see,' or, often painfully, feel and know to be true."[4] Reference to Pauline Smith's biography will show that her own experience has clearly gone into the creation of Niccoline Johanna. For Andrina also she has drawn on things which happened to her.

It has been shown how the Little Karoo farm, Mill River, with its old farmhouse and adjacent garden, is the original for Harmonie in *The Beadle*. During her visits to that farm, recorded in the *South African Journal*, Pauline Smith spent many hours in the garden near the homestead, went on a visit to the mill to fetch a thank-offering for the Dank Feast from the man who gave her the idea for Andries Lombard, and waited anxiously for the sacrament service. These experiences she used for her novel. Like her creator, Andrina spends long hours in the garden, goes up to the mill to fetch biscuits, and waits anxiously for the service which will admit her to the church.

Pauline Smith identifies herself so closely with Andrina du Toit that she goes as far as to put her own religious ideas into Andrina's mind. After she has been spoken to by the Pastor, the young woman thinks that she could understand a human Jesus who had made the sacrifice of everlasting death for other people. But she cannot understand or appreciate the sacrifice of a God who already knew he would rise from the dead on the third day. Andrina, however, is created to fit into a conservative and Godfearing society. And she is shown to be simple and accepting, the one person in *The Beadle* who is most completely in accord with herself and her environment. Is it likely that this person would have what would be for her such daring and iconoclastic religious thoughts? They are out of keeping with Andrina's other characteristics. Pauline Smith has identified herself too closely with the character; as a result Andrina reflects the inconsistency which lies in her thought and imagination. The other characters, who are moulded entirely by her artistic powers, do not suffer in this way. In Andrina's case the authoress's personal attachment to the character has blurred her art.

In "Why and How I became an Author" Pauline Smith writes:

I can remember no remarkable or precocious plunge into authorship in my childhood. It was in fact only slowly, through years of ill-health, that I came to write at all, and though ill-health may have made me a little more sensitive and impressionable than other robuster children, it did not make me an imaginative genius.[5]

She always seems to know what she can do in her writing and what lies beyond her powers. This knowledge of herself and of her ability is evident in this extract from a very honest article. She realised that the number of themes which could fire her imagination was few. She does not have the versatility and strength to impose her own vision upon a thousand different things as a more potent and inventive writer would be able to do. Rather she must wait for what has moved her to form itself in her mind and emotions. Her energy fades when she wanders from the Little Karoo district. Even there she deals with a limited number of topics. Self-righteousness and forgiveness, adversity and pain appear again and again with a certain sombre tone in her short stories. Her poetic symbolism, though telling, works within a fairly small range.

In her confined scope, in her awareness of her own limitations and in her impartial characterisation she suggests Jane Austen, although her work has nothing to do with the manners of a highly polished society or with urbanity. She is at her best in the creation of characters who are simple, comparatively inarticulate on account of poor education, but spiritually intense.

There is a clarity of line and a fine static quality about her work which leads the reader to compare her with the Greek artists who painted the ordered and eloquent shadows of soldiers, women, shepherds, and workmen upon the red and black clay of their vases. In her best work the red earth of the farmers' land is always in the background, giving an added stature and significance to the men and women who walk upon it.

CHAPTER 14

Lonely Places and a Past Generation

OCCASIONALLY one encounters adverse criticisms of Pauline Smith's work. These comments usually refer to her "sentimentality" or "unreal characters." This example comes from a book review of *South African Short Stories* edited by D. Wright.[1] Commenting on the editor's selection, the reviewer writes: "In pathetic contrast, the unsophisticated stories about rural characters (here a list is given including "The Pain". . .) are sentimental and dated and make this anthology, published in 1960, appear an anachronism."

Possibly this change in attitude is due to the fact that lovers of literature have had their sensibilities modified by a city existence. Simplicity of character, forthrightness, slowness of speech and action are not normally the qualities of city men and women. As a result, the reader either cannot believe these qualities when he sees them portrayed or he becomes suspicious of the author's motives.

Although Pauline Smith's writing has become generally known only recently, she is not a modern writer. In many respects she is closer to the Victorian age than to this generation. She would have known a world which was socially and economically stable. The houses in which she spent her younger years were furnished with sombre and heavy articles. Net and velvet curtains hung at the windows; family portraits were on the walls. Hers was a world of politeness and restraint.

Even when she was writing in the 1910's and 1920's, it is clear that she was thinking back to some earlier period, probably around the time of her own childhood. Her *South African Journal* of 1913-14 shows that she had many disappointments when she found that Little Karoo places and customs had changed—were no longer as in her girlish days. Fewer *takhaar* farmers were riding into Oudtshoorn for the thanksgiving service which celebrated the Boers' victory over the Zulus at Blood River.

The motor-car was beginning to supplant the ox-wagon, and journeys from one part of the Little Karoo to the other were becoming swifter and easier. As a result, the remote settlements were being opened up. When Pauline Smith was moved so greatly by the sacrament service at Mill River—an event she was to use so powerfully in her creative work—she comments in her journal that even that was something which was passing away.

Descriptions in the journal show that some of the farm buildings at Mill River were burnt and broken down by invading Afrikaner commandos in the South African War of 1899-1902.[2] In *The Beadle* the farm is created in its unharmed splendour as Harmonie. This is another more positive suggestion that Pauline Smith was looking back to a time before 1899 in which to set her novel. Her work is nearer in era to that of Olive Schreiner and Thomas Hardy than any of the modern writers. W. B. Yeats, who died in 1939, twenty years before her, is more modern. In a 1921 collection of verse he wrote:

> Things fall apart; the centre cannot hold;
> Mere anarchy is loosed upon the world.[3]

Pauline Smith had no interest in reflecting this violent intrusion of the twentieth century in her work. It is possible that she was largely insensitive to it. While "the ceremony of innocence"[4] was being drowned in Europe, she remained in the seclusion of her English cottage, dreaming of an earlier time. There she went on creating her simple characters, setting their fates and passions in the isolated world of the Little Karoo. Mr. Jack Cope, the South African novelist, describes the Little Karoo of her work as "a distilled crystal of her own creation . . . which remains utterly valid and penetrates through time and changed historical and other circumstances."

There are other ways in which Pauline Smith is closer to a past generation, for instance in the unshakeable moral framework of her writing. Although she is tolerant, sketching all her characters with an unbiased pen and a carefully controlled passion, her conception of a just order remains. Her stories are set in a definite world; she is neither fluid nor uncertain.

Prof. B. Mackenzie, a student of South African literature, points out that *The Beadle* contains an element of the popular, romantic novel of Victorian times in the story of the innocent heroine (Andrina) seduced by a callous and sophisticated villain (Henry Nind). The scene in which Andrina is actually seduced by the Englishman is not of the best in the book. Nind's suggestions to the girl are theatrical, somewhat unreal. Speaking in the third person, he says: "He wants to make you happier than you've even been before. He wants to bring your love to its fulfilment. And he thinks he could. Shall he risk it, Andrina?"[5] Finally, Andrina is won over, so innocent that she does not really know what is going on. The authoress comments, rather inadequately, "Klaartje's Andrina, to her peril, possessed no saving sense of sin."[6]

Pauline Smith's slowness of pace stems also from another age. Juriaan and Deltje van Royen live in quite content for fifty years together in the mountains. Ox-wagons take weeks to traverse short distances. Events ripen into climaxes as slowly as the crops on the earth. Silence, resignation, and patience are prominent characteristics of her men and women.

For all these reasons it is difficult for city readers to appreciate these stories. Their lives are dominated by hectic action and fear of the Bomb. The quietness and patience of the van Royens may seem idyllic and unreal. Pauline Smith's rigorous moral framework possibly strikes them as being too simple. Her leisureliness may frustrate and annoy them.

This difference must be admitted. But one way of life does not disqualify another. Fashion must not be mistaken for the only possible form of existence. The charge of sentimentality can be supported only by examining her presentation and characters on their own terms. Does Pauline Smith fight shy of realities such as disease, imperfection, frustration, and mischance for the sake of presenting a pretty and facile picture? Previous chapters have shown that this is not so. In her own gentle and often sombre way she is concerned with presenting the truth about human nature. Although there is no cynicism or "hard-boiled realism" in her style, it is nonetheless real.

CHAPTER 15

Pauline Smith and Olive Schreiner

ONE CANNOT think of Pauline Smith's work for long without calling to mind *The Story of an African Farm* by Olive Schreiner. This moody, inspired, egocentric woman spent the early years of her life as a governess on an isolated farm in the Great Karoo. She had received little education, was surrounded by rustic people who spoke only Afrikaans, and was cut off from books and conversation. During those years she yearned to improve herself. She must have felt that she was buried before her time, and the frustration, like the irritant which produces the pearl in the oyster, caused her to write this imaginative, self-revealing novel.

Pauline Smith shows how solitariness develops the religious, contemplative faculties in her characters. Olive Schreiner moves even closer and gives the reader long, descriptive insights into the thoughts and imaginings of Waldo and Lyndall, who have been brought up on a lonely Karoo farm. These characters are two aspects of the author's own spirit. Lyndall is proud, moodily impatient of the restraints which are placed upon women in her society, and constantly in search of something perfect on which she can shower her love and adoration. Waldo is impressed by the mystery of the world. He is conscious always of the stars, of their remoteness and brightness. He wishes at all costs *to know*: why the great boulders have been piled together on the plains to form the Karoo *koppies;* why there are similar patterns in the outline of a tree in winter and in the veins which cover the entrails of a gander.

In his biography of his wife, S. C. Cronwright-Schreiner writes:

When more than ordinarily excited she would rush up and down with short, quick, agitated, yet almost heavy steps, throwing her apparently short arms in the air, shaking them above her head, banging the sides of her head or of her body violently with her fists; . . . alternately she would shake her hands in the air at her sides with such force and rapidity that her fingers used to click together rapidly and loudly.[1]

There are many other examples of Olive's excitability. She suffered through her life from nervous asthma and could not stay in one place for any length of time. Her book is invested with this intense nervous energy. Reading it evokes in one a kind of yearning restlessness.

In Pauline Smith the emotions do not reach this degree of rawness. Although old Alie van Staden of "Desolation" is turned out of her home, compelled to cross a drought-stricken wilderness, and dies after she had been separated from her grandson, the reader is not stirred up into turbulent indignation or thrown into the depths of despair. Alie's dream of finding work with the mattress-maker at Tan' Betje's house is not stripped from her. "Up some other lane it must be, but she would find it. A little house with green shutters and a pear-tree in the yard. . . ."[2] She dies plucking the imaginary coir with her fingers. Somehow one's feelings are brought into harmony by knowing this woman's hard end. Her dignity brings one a willingness to accept.

Olive Schreiner's intense religious speculations make her novel feverish and sad. She was the daughter of Gottlieb, a religious and gentle-hearted German, who came out to South Africa as a missionary. His simple ways and unquestioning faith are portrayed in the character of old Otto, the German overseer, in the novel. Olive inherited his capacity for love and his desire for supernatural reality. But her brilliant mind quickly absorbed the prevailing skepticism of the late nineteenth century. How could God have created the world and placed man and the animals in the Garden of Eden at some given time when geology showed that the rocks had been laid down hundred of millions of years ago, and that strange beasts had lived in those early aeons? Was it possible to speak about a soul when thoughts and emotions were caused by changes in the chemicals of the body?

Science would find out all things, and nowhere in the great
rational plan would there be a place for a God to survive. With
her heart Olive Schreiner wanted God; yet her mind told her
that he could not be. There would be no continued existence
for those that she loved after they had died. These thoughts
brought her anguish, as they did to Tennyson, Matthew Arnold,
and Thomas Hardy. *The Story of an African Farm* shows a con-
tinual shifting of position, as if Olive were uncertain which
spoke more truth, her emotions or her brain.

When Waldo hears of the death of Lyndall, he tries to face
squarely the fact that she is annihilated.

He looked up into the night sky that all his life long had mingled
itself with his existence. There were a thousand faces that he loved
looking down at him, a thousand stars in their glory, in crowns and
circles, and solitary grandeur; . . . yet he looked up at them and
shuddered; at last turned away from them with horror. Such count-
less multitudes stretching out far into space, and yet not in one of
them all was she! Though he searched through them all, to the
farthest, faintest point of light, nowhere should he ever say "She is
here!". . . He saw before him the long ages of eternity that would
roll on, on, on, and never bring her. She would exist no more. A dark
mist filled the room.

"Oh, little hand! oh, little voice! oh, little form!" he cried; "oh, little
soul that walked with mine; oh, little soul, that looked so fearlessly
down into the depths, do you exist no more for ever—for all time?"[3]

The style is imaginative, tense, and restless. It seems to proceed
from an urgent need to communicate rather than from careful
consideration, as in Pauline Smith. Waldo's words are un-
controlled and border on hysteria. This fear that life is likely
to be snuffed out leads to Olive Schreiner's intensely felt vision
of the meaninglessness of existence and of the loneliness of the
individual. When still a boy, Waldo invented a machine for
shearing sheep. This was the joy of his heart, and speculating
on how it would succeed brought him many comforting dreams.
After Old Otto, his father, died, the machine was destroyed by
the repulsive bully and swindler, Bonaparte Blenkins. While
the boy huddles over the broken implement, his dog runs off to
discover by chance a beetle in the veld. In the ensuing descrip-

tion, Olive Schreiner provides a comment on life both human and animal.

> He walked off to play with a black-beetle. The beetle was hard at work trying to roll home a great ball of dung it had been collecting all the morning; but Doss broke the ball, and ate the beetle's hind-legs, and then bit off its head. And it was all play and no one could tell what it had lived and worked for. A striving, and a striving, and an ending in nothing.[4]

As the thought of Lyndall's nonexistence torments him, Waldo thinks of the theories usually advanced to explain away death. He rejects the conventional Christian idea, because it tells him that Lyndall died proud without asking mercy of God, and by rights she should be in Hell. The more optimistic nineteenth-century idea of God the all-loving is also inadequate, as is the Transcendentalists' notion of the eternal soul. Waldo wants to see Lyndall as she was, an earthly woman; otherwise not at all. Truth is the most difficult to accept. The man who would serve it not only has to cast away the comfortable illusions of conventional religion; he is also forced into isolation by his fellows.

This desire for truth at all costs is another quality which brings pride, pain and sadness to *The Story of an African Farm*. As a girl Lyndall wishes to get away from the constraining atmosphere of the farm. She is contrasted against Em who is accepting and conventional. When the two are threading beads Lyndall is the more skilled. Em asks her why her beads never come off the needle. In Lyndall's reply one notices the independence and determination which are to characterise her life. "'I try,' said the little one gravely, moistening her tiny finger. 'That is why.'"[5] Later, the German overseer is dismissed by Tant Sannie and the two girls are locked in their room so that they cannot go to him. Em wails despairingly, but Lyndall does her utmost to get out of the heavily shuttered window before retiring silently to bed. Only you can help yourself and you must never surrender, is her philosophy. She admires Napoleon Bonaparte because "he was one man, only one . . . yet all the people in the world feared him. He was not born great, he was common as we are; yet he was master of the world at last. . . . When he said a thing to himself he never forgot it."[6] Lyndall's admiration for Napoleon is a hero-worship of the "superman." Waldo is surprised that she can understand how he thought and felt. This shows that the young girl identifies herself with him.

A characteristic of this desire for perfection is a restlessness with the accidents and limitations of real life. Lyndall achieves her desire to escape from the farm and to go to boarding school, only to find that life there is also ignorant and wrong-headed. On her return to the farm she pours out to Waldo her indignation at the role of women in society. It is a sign of her aspiring spirit that she frets even against the fact that environment has a power in moulding the individual from childhood. "We all enter the world little plastic beings, with so much natural force, perhaps, but for the rest—blank; and the world tells us what we are to be, and shapes us by the ends it puts before us."[7]

In her search for the perfect being she has formed an alliance with a man by whom she has conceived a child. He fetches her away from the farm and repeatedly offers to marry her. She rejects this because she fears that he will tread her down like an ordinary woman. Attended only by a servant, she comes to an up-country boarding house where the child is born. It dies almost immediately and she herself grows ill. Her last words to Gregory Rose, an admirer who followed her and was now acting as her nurse, display the tragic conflict between her warm, womanly emotions and her proud, heroic mind which still pursued that ideal and intangible truth. The conflict is centred round her child.

"It was so small," she said; "it lived such a little while—only three hours. They laid it close by me, but I never saw it; I could feel it by me." She waited: "Its feet were so cold; I took them in my hand to make them warm, and my hand closed right over them, they were so little." There was an uneven trembling in her voice. "It crept close to me; it wanted to drink, it wanted to be warm." She hardened herself—"I did not love it; its father was not my prince; I did not care for it; but it was so little." She moved her hand. "They might have kissed it, one of them, before they put it in. It never did any one any harm in all its little life. They might have kissed it, one of them."[8]

The intense emotion, and the reader's realisation that Lyndall's own proud, aspiring nature has brought her to this pass make the passage like a nightmare. He returns to the less intense world of everyday with a sigh of relief.

Waldo also pursues his ideal of truth. The allegory told to him by the stranger who visits the farm is supposed to brace the spirits and to elevate the will so that a man can be inspired to seek out reality at all costs. Certainly the great, bald mountains which the hunter after truth assaults are clear and magnificent. But he leaves behind the beautiful birds of Immortality and Reward-after-Death with such regret that sadness almost outweighs his newfound resolution. The cliffs which he climbs in solitude are bathed in sunlight, but the going is hard. There is something of the nightmare here also. Human bones lie in places, blood oozes from the hunter's fingers, and wild faces poke out of the holes in the rock to yell at him. Ravaged by age and overwork, he can go on no longer. He lies down, and, gazing below, sees for a moment the trees and fields of his childhood. "From afar seemed borne to him the cry of his own wild birds, and he heard the noise of people singing as they danced. And he thought he heard amongst them the voices of his old comrades; and he saw far off the sunlight shine on his early home. And great tears gathered in the hunter's eyes."[9]

The pursuit of truth may be heroic, but it takes a man into gloomy and despairing regions from which he longs to escape by accepting everyday life with all its imperfections and frustrations. As the hunter's eyes close, a feather drops onto his breast from the elusive bird of truth. The "feather" comes to the dying Lyndall in the form of a vision. In her final sickness she says: "I can see the vision of a poor weak soul striving after good. It was not cut short; and, in the end, it learnt through tears and such pain, that holiness is an infinite compassion for others; that greatness is to take the common things of life and walk truly among them."[10] This idea is restated more strongly in the last chapter of the book; one which in its quiet serenity follows surprisingly on the agonised soul-searchings which precede it. Waldo goes out to sit in the sun and enjoy the beauty of the scene. Olive Schreiner seems to have forgotten that she has questioned the existence of God. Here it is taken for granted. She writes "Beauty is God's wine, with which he recompenses the souls that love him; he makes them drunk."[11]

After Lyndall's death, Waldo has attained a measure of peace by thinking that she had entered the universal life—the philosophy which sees the beloved person still present in tree and sky and in the cycle of nature. But in this last scene his state is still more joyful. It seems to consist in accepting life just as it is, without too much wondering or trying to find out the answers. He feels that life is rich and good.

Waldo, as he sat with his knees drawn up to his chin and his arms folded on them, looked at it all and smiled. An evil world . . . it might be; but a lovely world for all that, and to sit there gloating in the sunlight was perfect. It was worth having been a little child, and having cried and prayed, so one might sit there. He moved his hands as though he were washing them in the sunshine. There will always be something worth living for while there are shimmery afternoons.[12]

This analysis shows that Olive Schreiner had an intense religious concern which is beyond the scope of Pauline Smith. In her journal the latter recounts a conversation she had with Thys Taute. He confesses to her that he finds it hard to believe in Christ. She comments: "Sitting round the fire we got to feel I think like two sinners shut out of Heaven by the predikant. If the predikant would preach the humanity of Christ, not the Divinity, take him for a peasant teacher instead of the Son of God, perhaps they would do more for sinners like Thys and me and most of the rest of the world."[13] In *The Beadle* Andrina also expresses this preference for a human Christ. "If Christ had been but the son of Joseph, not of God, if He had died not to rise again, but to lie forever in the grave, then, thought Andrina, she could have understood and loved Him."[14]

Pauline Smith seems to accept the implication of these ideas, i.e., annihilation after death, with a greater equanimity than Olive Schreiner could ever achieve. She is not as intellectual as Olive and does not worry at the subject all the time. Neither is she as consistent. In her writing she often skirts the problem, portraying the faith of Godfearing, conventional people who do not question. The old van der Merwes of Harmonie, Niklaas Dampers (the sinner), Ludovitje who converted Maqwasi the Kaffir, and the Steenkamp sisters all believe as they have been taught. Pauline Smith shows that for the van der Merwes and Ludovitje at least, faith is an ennobling and comely thing.

Biographical details show that the two authoresses were different in temperament. Olive Schreiner was vital, dominating, and in constant, restless pursuit of self-knowledge. Her husband, who took *her* name at the time of their marriage, confesses that she was the most energetic and incisive arguer he had ever encountered.

I can still see the dear little woman . . . at her best, just life and force and brilliancy personified, sitting in a Madeira chair with one leg doubled under her at times, hammering the arms of the chair with her little fists, and everybody chuckling as her thrusts got home. It was a great fight; the blood surges and throbs through my veins even now as I recall it.[15]

Pauline, on the other hand, was retiring and lacking in self-confidence. As a child she looked to her father for guidance. In her later life Arnold Bennett had to bully and encourage her constantly before she could write. She seemed not to be able to trust her own thoughts and feelings until somebody else had given them a kind of informal "Imprimatur" and "Nihil Obstat." When Bennett died, and there was no one to goad her on, her writings came to an end.

A glance through Olive Schreiner's letters shows how self-revealing and self-concerned they are. She was so honest about herself and her comments were so penetrating that the English author and psychologist, Havelock Ellis, found her an ideal subject for observation. On December 14, 1888, she writes to ask him.

Havelock, don't you know of anything I could take to strengthen my nerves? It's no good taking bromide; it simply weakens one yet further. What is given for hysteria? (Awful sensitiveness in lower part of body). Isn't valerian a good thing?[16]

Many years later she writes to her husband.

Very hot and oppressive, but I have to keep the fire going to dry the air. . . . Oh, I wish I could get my book [*From Man to Man*] done before I die. It may not be any good; but I feel I have to do it. I used to feel I couldn't die till it was done; that fate wouldn't let it be. Now I know that anything may be; you trust and hope for years but the things never come.[17]

There are many others in this vein. Often she reveals her innermost feelings frankly and at length. She worries at religious and social problems, striving to attain a mental and emotional equilibrium.

Pauline Smith's letters and journal do not display as much self-analysis. She feels, but does not dwell on her feelings, and her concern is as much for others as for herself. Her *South African Journal* of 1913-14 was kept only at the insistence of Arnold Bennett. It presents a gallery of widely different characters. One gains the impression that she is deeply interested in the everyday details of the lives of those she met. She records the kind of clothes they wore, their difficulties with luggage, illness, tiredness, and so on. She tends always to look outwards, while Olive looks in at her own being. Olive inclines to the "egotistical sublime," while Pauline, like Keats, has more of the "chameleon" in her nature. When concentrating upon a person's life story, she is inclined to lose consciousness of self, and to identify herself with him and it.

Both authors have given a character to the empty, parched central plateau of South Africa in their stories. In "Desolation" Pauline Smith gives a description of the cruelty, stoniness, and vastness of the Karoo which is compelling and accurate. Three short stories set in the Aangenaam Valley district of the Little Karoo tend to show a veld which is more picturesque. The beautiful colours on the mountains at dawn and dusk are stressed. The Harmonie farmhouse runs some little danger of becoming the "Old Cape Dutch Homestead" of the picture calendar or the biscuit-tin lid. It is only the truthfulness of Pauline Smith's simple vision which saves this idealised scene from toppling into the realm of wishful-thinking and sentimentality. Olive Schreiner's farmhouse in *The Story of an African Farm* is rough and broken-down. Her Karoo is harshly realistic—heat, dust, hunger, crude prickly pears—and at the same time old and mysterious.

As a literary artist Pauline Smith is probably the more successful. She could see people and things more objectively. Her common sense is stronger, and she wrote slowly, carefully, and with great deliberation. Olive has the more powerful imagination and the more lurid, intense personality. A fitting symbol for her life as an artist can perhaps be found in the hunter after truth who followed his elusive bird into the solitude of the great mountains. Roy Campbell discerned the appropriateness of this when he climbed up to her tomb at Buffel's Kop, a great, stark *koppie* overlooking the Karoo town of Cradock. In a short poem he recounts his feelings:

> the gloom
> Moving one way; all heaven in the gale
> Roaring: and high above the insulted tomb
> An eagle anchored on full spread of sail
> That from its wings let fall a silver plume.[18]

How is the life of Pauline Smith to be symbolised? One tends to think of Niccoline Johanna, the pastor's daughter, who endured so many blows of fate, and perhaps even more of old Alie van Staden, who retained her dignity even in a time of drought and death. If Olive Schreiner suggests aspiration, dreams, and ardent striving, Pauline Smith brings to one the thoughts of quietness and patience.

CHAPTER 16

A Love for the Individual—H. C. Bosman, Uys Krige and Pauline Smith Compared

TWO OTHER South African writers are to be represented in this series—H. C. Bosman and Uys Krige. Like Pauline Smith, both have dealt with the South African scene in their work. Unlike her, both are Afrikaners themselves.

Bosman's life was as full of action and crisis as hers was uneventful. At an early age he killed his half-brother after a dispute, and was sentenced to death. This was later commuted to ten years' imprisonment. The horror of being under sentence and the rigours and crudities of prison life are startlingly revealed in his novel, *Cold Stone Jug*. His descriptions of his time in the death cell leave the reader with feelings of depression and emptiness. In the shadow of the gallows "a jest or a solemn speech meant just about the same thing."[1] Finally the day arrives for his companion, Stoffels, to be hanged. Bosman describes the event with a kind of devastating sarcasm and mordant humor.

No orders had to be given. Each man knew what was expected of him, even Stoffels,—who played his part tolerably well, considering the fact that he was not rehearsed in it and was getting no pay for it.[2]

Stark realism follows; the sounds of scuffles and footfalls. From the cell to which he has been removed, Bosman hears Stoffels's voice, but he has difficulty in recognising it: "for only part of that noise seemed to come out of his throat. The rest of it seemed to have come out of his belly."[3] Then the slam of the trap-door shakes the whole building, and, the dreadful event over, the prison starts the business of the day.

Bosman reveals a ready sympathy for the most hardened and hopeless of the convicts—those serving the indeterminate sentence, a system whereby they could be kept in jail indefinitely. In the prison they were called "blue-coats" on account of their distinctive dress. Their language was as colourful as their careers during the comparatively short spells that they were out of "boob." To Bosman they told the inside stories of burglaries which they had committed. He re-creates these with gusto, reproducing the "boob slang" in which they were originally related.

The other prisoners thought that he was mad to associate with these hardened types, and took it as an indication of his criminal tendencies. Actually his imagination enabled him to understand their problems, while his sensitivity and heart caused him to identify himself with them. Pauline Smith showed similar qualities when she interested herself in the *bywoner* class and the poor Whites in the Little Karoo. This interest was contrary to the general attitude of the Oudtshoorners amongst whom she moved. "I could never understand why Pauline Smith was interested in those people. They are stupid; they won't work; they're lazy," an acquaintance related. As with Bosman, the artistic imagination strips away the prejudice to see the characters for what, in reality, they are.

Cold Stone Jug also contains a frank discussion of sexual matters—the homosexuality which is widespread amongst the prisoners, the dreams of the prisoner, Huysmans, for Tossie, a twelve-year-old girl whom he had seduced in his class at school. Bosman confesses to his own longings and frustrations. This is a department of writing which is beyond Pauline Smith's experience and scope. She belongs to a more reticent and decorous school. But she never shies away from the reality and strength of sexual relationships. The hold of Jacoba Nooi upon Niklaas Dampers, and the violence of the young girl's passion for Jan Boetje in "The Schoolmaster" are well-portrayed. They are achieved, however, by implication and careful emotive writing rather than by presentation of (to quote a phrase of Bosman) "juicy details."

Bosman moves beyond the range of Pauline Smith in his analysis of frenzied states either bordering on or of outright madness. He describes how at one stage he had the nightmare notion of different kinds of animals propagating. "A pig and a rooster would have sexual intercourse: and the offspring they would produce would be half pig, half rooster. A snout and a comb, and a curly tail and feathers. And pigs' trotters with spurs."[4]

Later he is taken to the prison doctor and is able to convince him that he is still sane. But on his return to his cell he is again swept by these moods of insanity. The urge takes him to crawl on all fours around the concrete floor. In his madness he retains a "strange cunning,"[5] and times the visits of the warders, ensuring that they will never surprise him in this compromising position. These descriptions remind the reader of descriptions of the deranged mind in the work of Edgar Allan Poe.

Cold Stone Jug is inclined to be repetitious. It conveys harsh and unpleasant experience with an incisive realism and caustic wit, which are far removed from the highly formal and carefully created effects of Pauline Smith.

Before Bosman was jailed, he had spent a short time schoolmastering in the Marico district of the Northwestern Transvaal. This region had a relatively sparse population of farmers; down-to-earth, rustic characters who spoke Afrikaans and remembered with emotion the days of the independent Boer Republic. Their sense of humour was broad and crude. They loved practical jokes. The everyday realities of running a farm and fighting against drought were uppermost in their minds, and persistently entered their conversations. Love, violence, and anecdotes from the Anglo-Boer War of 1899-1902 formed the subjects of their stories.

Bosman drew heavily on this material and created a unique character and atmosphere in the short stories first collected under the title *Mafeking Road*. Recently further stories in this series have been published in the book *Unto Dust*.

The principal character is Oom Schalk Lourens, a wily, good-natured farmer who acts as the storyteller for most of the tales. They range from highly lyrical love stories (e.g., "The Veld Maiden") to accounts of grim reality, privation, and human endurance ("The Rooinek").[6]

Humour also plays an important part. Bosman frequently makes skilful use of incident to show the weaknesses and prejudices in the farmer's view of life. For instance, "Unto Dust" tells of the death of a burgher, Hans Welman. Hans was speared by a "Kafir" in a skirmish and his friend, Stoffel Oosthuizen, was so angered to see it happen that he reined in his horse at great danger to himself and took a potshot at the murderer. His bullet found its mark. Later, he went back to collect Welman's remains for a Christian burial. To his chagrin he found that the disjointed skeletons of the "Kafir" and his friend were inextricably mixed. Stoffel shooed away a yellow dog which had belonged to the "Kafir" and was still keeping vigil over its master's remains, and sorted out the bones as best he could. He was intensely irritated. For him death was not the great leveller. Such an idea "sounded like out of a speech made by one of those liberal Cape politicians."[7] When he had finished, he carted Hans Welman's bones to his farm and buried them in the graveyard. But some time later the faithful yellow dog was found squatting on the mound of the farmer's grave!

Bosman loves to tell a story which is carefully contrived, which will show up the stupidity of prejudice in a humorous and tolerant manner, and which contains an energetic and incisive twist at the conclusion. In his volume of essays, *A Cask of Jerepigo*, he expresses an admiration for O. Henry. He bears a resemblance to this writer in the taut manipulation of plot and in the use of the surprise ending.

Another humorous effect is gained when Bosman shows the reader that his (Bosman's) sympathy for the "Kafir" and understanding of the situation extend beyond that of the Marico farmers who are his characters. The Afrikaners acknowledge that Radipalong, a Bechuana wood-carver, is skilful in carving animals.

He could carve a hippopotamus, or a rhinoceros, or an elephant, or a yellow-bellied hyena—the more low sort of hyena—in such a way that you *knew* that animal exactly, through your having seen it grazing under a tree, or drinking at a water-hole, or just leaning against an anthill, without doing anything in particular.[8]

But when he gets onto carving likenesses of the farmers, they will not admit that he has the same cunning. They buy these carvings "just for fun,"[9] and they laugh in embarrassment—both signs that they have recognised the skill of the work. Yet Radipalong remains "a lazy Bechuana, who would have been better employed in chopping up that wood and bringing a bundle of it into a farmer's kitchen."[10] By means of the plot Bosman makes the reader understand that these carvings are very apt. It is only after she has seen Radipalong's carving of her fiancé, Karel Nienaber, that Louisa Wessels breaks off her engagement. Again this story has a sting in the tail. Most of it is written in a bantering and comic style. But at the end the reader is told that Nienaber left the Marico bushveld soon after the engagement was broken off, because he saw in Louisa's trousseau kist his own image with several rusty nails driven into the heart. With a sudden contrast Bosman moves from laughter to the grim world of witchcraft.

Other stories deal with heroism, fidelity, and endurance against unconquerable odds. "The Rooinek" tells of a trek into the Kalahari Desert which for one ox-wagon and its passengers ends in death. Gradually, Oom Schalk and his friends come to respect the Englishman, Webber, who had started to farm in the Marico district. He becomes friendly with Koos Steyn in particular, and when Koos alone decides to cross the Kalahari with his family, accompanies him. Koos has a daughter, Jemima, who was the Englishman's favourite. Later Webber's body is discovered. In his last, thirst-crazed moments he must have imagined that he was carrying the girl. Oom Schalk relates: "When we lifted his body, we found, still clasped in his dead and rigid arms, a few old rags and a child's clothes."[11]

The pathos in "The Rooinek" is strong and genuine. On occasions Bosman is liable to grow sentimental; but these are to be found in his lighter love stories when he describes beautiful, young girls. Whenever he portrays death as a result of war

("Makapan's Caves") or passion ("The Gramophone" and "The Widow") his writing conveys an intense energy.

Clearly these stories invite comparison with Pauline Smith's *Little Karoo*. Both authors have been concerned in capturing the spirit of a relatively isolated community. Also, there are certain similarities in the temperaments of the men and women who provide their subject matter. The dwellers in the Marico and those in the Little Karoo share a brooding, intense spirit. They are liable to be violent. They are superstitious. God looms large in their thoughts. Mintje Lombard, wife of Andries in "The Miller," tramps sixteen miles down the Aangenaam Valley to fetch an eelskin which she believes will cure her husband of his cough. Oom Schalk Lourens's father pays a visit to a "Kafir" witch-doctor with his friend, Paul Kruger.[12]

Both regions are subject to drought, when the spirit of endurance of the inhabitants is tested to the utmost. It is instructive to compare Pauline Smith's story of old Alie van Staden who trekked across the Verlatenheid with her grandson in search of the Hermansdorp of her memories, with Bosman's "The Rooinek." His description of the trek into the Kalahari Desert contains a compelling realism. He shows himself interested in the question of leadership. What makes the other trekkers follow Gerhardhus Grobbelaar, and why does he lose his authority in the end? Finally there is a portrayal of courage and the ultimate helplessness of men in the face of adverse elements. Pauline Smith presents the realities of drought as convincingly. But her treatment of Alie van Staden is more tender. She works her way into the depths of the decrepit *bywoner's* thoughts and feelings. She identifies herself with Alie up to the moment of her death. Bosman, on the other hand tends to present the deaths in the desert as a grim, real, and moving spectacle. He sees the characters from the outside —the reader watches them expiring. There is an element of cruelty in the way Bosman presents a tragic incident to the reader: "Look at it: face up to it," he seems to say. "See if you can take it like I can."

Generally, Bosman and Pauline Smith have a different emphasis. He presents humorous and absurd situations with a vision which is beyond her range. He has a strong satirical leaning which leads him to regard human failings as objects of amusement. She sees weaknesses with a tender sympathy. Although there is humour in her work, it is not accompanied by the satiric tang, which at times attains the dimensions of devastating cynicism in Bosman's work.

By the power of her imagination Pauline Smith transmutes the Little Karoo into a new and isolated world. The reader sees the characters moving against the backdrop of the mountains and in the fields as in a picture which bears many resemblances to, but is remote from the everyday. Bosman is much nearer to the Marico bushveld. It is not distanced (as the Karoo is for Pauline) by 6,000 miles of sea; neither is it a district associated with the cherished and luminous memories of childhood.

Uys Krige is an author of considerable reputation in this country. Much of his writing is in Afrikaans, but he has also produced plays, short stories, and a war book in English. He has an excellent command of the language, with a poet's love for idioms and for descriptive and unusual words. To those South Africans born and brought up in the Western district of the Cape Province he speaks with particular intensity. Here there is no great gulf fixed between the English- and Afrikaans-speaking South Africans. Many are equally familiar with both languages. Neither is there complete separation of the European and Coloured people. It is a colourful and healthy region of oceans, mountains, and magnificent flora.

Uys Krige re-creates this atmosphere with warmth and light. In "The Dream," a long, autobiographical story,[13] he tells of Jannie Kotze's pride when he hears from his mother that he is to have a baby brother. Now he will have someone to call *Kleinboet* (little brother); and the new child will respond by referring to him as *Ouboet* (big brother). Thus his definite superiority will be established over his other brothers, Kosie and Pieter, who are so near him in age. Jannie is a sensitive and spirited child. His attachment to his mother is strong and simple. He responds powerfully to the rich, subtle atmosphere of the Western Cape village of Stellenbosch and the nearby coastline. One year the Kotze family go on holiday to Onrust, a seaside resort.

[164]

A Love for the Individual

They had had a wonderful time on the beach. They had swum in the breakers foaming blue and white about them; run about on the white sands; collected coloured shells; scrambled on to the huge rocks; gazed into rockpools full of starfish, slowly waving sea-plants and green and gold *klipvissies* drifting lazily from crevice to crevice—with here and there a small, red crab staring at them out of its beady eyes through the still clear water.[14]

After the baby is born, Jannie is sent away to friends of the family in Claremont, a suburb of Cape Town. He has never been used to a sumptuous bathroom where hot water can be turned on at will. His eager young nature is greatly impressed. Every evening his Uncle Innes would throw some greenish crystals into the water.

And then Jannie would get into the steaming bath and lie there quite motionless in the sweet-smelling water, admiring the bathroom. It didn't only have light-blue tiles on the wall. It had them halfway up the wall. The bath, especially, was a miracle, . . . You didn't climb into it, you slipped into it as into a swimming-bath.[15]

Uys Krige's description of character is more exuberant than Pauline Smith's. He has the poet's eye for noticing and exaggerating predominant features. Nurse Leppan, who assisted at the confinement of Jannie's mother, "seemed to be both big and small at the same time. The head . . . appeared to have no neck, as if screwed onto the strong, broad shoulders. . . . Everything about her was impressive—the big nose, the red bulging cheeks with the skin smooth and taut as if the bone beneath were curved like a hoop."[16] Two long paragraphs are devoted to description of this person; a striking contrast to the brief, unemphatic descriptions to be found in Pauline Smith.

Fears of death and imaginings about it play a large part in Jannie's life. When still very young he had gone to the funeral of his grandfather, and remembers clearly looking down into the grave: "It was just at that moment—when except for one small corner the coffin's shiny lid had disappeared under the damp earth—that for the second time in his life Jannie had felt lost, utterly lost."[17] Death intruded itself again into his imagination and emotions when his Aunt Miemie and her daughters, Kathleen and Francina, had been drowned in a river. All these fears, together with images of the sea and of the red crab encountered in the pool at Onrust, reappear in a nightmare which comes to Jannie after his *Kleinboet's* death.

Uys Krige describes this dreadful experience with imaginative vigour. His writing is elemental. Many of the basic states of being—feelings of cosiness, happiness, loneliness, horror—are recreated; and this author has the ability to evoke an intense awareness of life in the reader. The narrative tends to ramble at times, but this is not out of place in the episodes of a child's life.

Published in the same volume with "The Dream" are four episodes dealing with war experience in the African desert and in Italy. Here Uys Krige conveys the cruelty, mutilations and ever-present death which come with fighting. "Death of the Zulu" is an intense, realistic description of a hopelessly wounded African who asks to be shot. There is a strong fellow-feeling for the courage of the man. "Two Daumiers" offers two vivid descriptions of the horrors of battle—the carbonised remains of Italians in a burnt-out tank, and a shot Basuto.

In "Christmas Box" Krige shows his instinctive love for life. It is Christmas Day in the Specialist Hospital at Naples. Ward C houses the worst cases, and in particular an Indian, Ranjat, whose face has been completely shot away. "Where there should have been a face, there was only a big, black hole. No eyes, no nose, no mouth, no lips."[18] This man has been losing the will to live, and the Chief Dental Surgeon, who tells the story, has grown jaded and despairing because of him. On Christmas Day a group of nuns bring presents to the mutilated men. Ward C grows lively and joyful. They put on a record of "Roll Out the Barrel," and each man responds in some way to the music. The dental surgeon comes into the ward and sees the Indian propped up in bed with the muslin cloth like a screen across his nonexistent face.

Calmly, peacefully, Ranjat's strong left hand rested on a flame-coloured, finely stitched handkerchief (from the nuns) while his right hand beat with his bare knuckles on the bedside table a triumphant tattoo in time to the music.[19]

[166]

At this assertion of life and humanity in the face of all adversity the spirit of the narrator soars.

The Way Out relates Uys Krige's experiences as an escaped prisoner of war in Italy. It is also an assertion of life—ordinary, everyday, sensible, human life—in the midst of the insanities, pettiness, and violence of warfare. The author shows love and admiration for the Italian peasants who risked their lives to shelter prisoners and to ferry them across the enemy lines. He appreciates their homeliness and the quietness of their minds. There are many lyrical descriptions of the Italian mountains, of forest scenes, and of the states of emotion which they induced in the author.

The Way Out has an impressive and startling epilogue. When Uys Krige and his associates have finally got through to their own armies, he is bitterly disappointed by the official attitude towards the Italians who had helped them. There is little warmth or consideration for the individual. The ex-prisoners of war spend an unpleasant time in the town of Foggia which was "like a surrealist's nightmare come true,"[20] after the Liberators had bombed large areas. Despairingly they loiter around the streets. A group of Cockney soldiers offer them tea in their temporary "head-quarters" in an old building. These men have taken a few Italian waifs under their wing. It is not until the escapees have listened to the lively banter of these ordinary, unimportant men that they feel faith and hope again.

Uys Krige has also written drama in English. "Fuente Sagrada," "The Sniper," and "All Roads Lead to Rome"[21] are set in wartime. In times like these life becomes extremely difficult. What is right and wrong when two armies converge on each other? How does the individual fight, blinding himself to the humanity of his enemies? Uys Krige shows great concern for suffering people in these plays and always comes out in favour of the individual before the theory or the mass ideal.

One of the key scenes of "Fuente Sagrada," a play of the Spanish Civil War, revolves around a peasant who comes onto the stage dragging a cart filled with his few possessions. Marais, a South African volunteer fighting for the Republicans, demands the cart to carry a box of army papers. He tries to persuade the peasant that the Republican government will put an end to all his woes.

Marais: So you don't know what your Government, the Government to whom that box belongs, is fighting for? That it's fighting for homes, water, land for all.

Peasant: I have a piece of land.

Marais: For doctors for you, hospitals.

Peasant: I have never been sick.

Marais: For teachers, schools.

Peasant: I don't need to read or write.

Marais: And your children?

Peasant: I am not married.[22]

The peasant is suspicious of all governments. All he knows is "Two armies attacked each other. I was in between."[23] Marais's idealism is all very well, but really it is only the individual lives which count.

The whole point of "The Sniper" is its concern for the individual and its recognition of common humanity. Captain Meyer, German-born but a South African citizen, takes two Germans prisoner in Italy. One of them, Otto Geyer, after thanking him for his chivalrous behaviour, is staggered to hear that Meyer is a Jew.

Geyer: Forgive me, *Herr Kapitän,* that I speak so candidly . . . but they presented the Jews to us in such a different light, I never dreamt that. . . .

Meyer: . . . we are ordinary normal human beings.[24]

Later, Colonel Venter, Meyer's fiery and efficient senior officer, wants to shoot the second German, Heinrich, because the man has killed his young godson, Liebenberg. Meyer tries to get it across to the Colonel that the German soldier is another young man, and as such deserves his sympathy.

Meyer: They're the same kind of people. They even look the same. Yes, Liebenberg could have been the German, and the German, Liebenberg.[25]

Colonel Venter taunts Meyer. The Captain is a Jew. Surely he, more than anyone else, should have a grievance against the

Germans for the extermination of millions of his race? Meyer replies, "I cannot blame an entire people—like the Nazis blamed an entire people."[26] Otherwise he is afraid he will become what he hates.

Uys Krige's stories do not have the careful planning and over-all structure which Pauline Smith gives to hers. His subject matter is much more varied. Like Bosman, he stands much closer to his characters and scenes than she does. In "The Coffin," a story set on a Cape farm, he begins by showing Great Oupa Lourens in a patriarchal light. On the morning that his first great-grandchild is born, the old man takes his whip and goes out into the veld, where he lashes around him in a muscular and assertive fashion. Soon, however, the reader is introduced to his humour and quaint language. Great Oupa calls the coffins at the undertaker's "black-sheep."[27] Another term for this item of furniture is "teak bed."[28] Uys Krige has shown the man in his lighter moments, and he loses the Old Testament status immediately. He becomes intensely human. In a certain sense Krige has a much closer understanding of the Afrikaans farmer. He does not stress the comparison with the Biblical atmosphere, and is more relaxed in the drawing of these characters.

There is one quality which these three writers have in common, whatever the differences of their subject matter and technique —a quality which gives energy, interest, and truth to their work. All three have a love for the individual. They do not make the mistake of thinking that an ideology, a conventional attitude of prejudice, or a philosophy are more important.

H. C. Bosman spends time with the blue-coats in the "boob," feeling for them and listening to their interminable stories, turning a deaf ear to the condemnations of his fellow "superior" prisoners. Pauline Smith sees a great deal in the poor labourers of the Little Karoo, although the circle in which she moves considers them a waste of time. Uys Krige discerns a common humanity in Zulu and Afrikaner, Italian, Spaniard, Coloured, and Englishman. These writers have the boldness to stand away from the common herd and there is independence in their vision.

CHAPTER 17

Some Opinions on Pauline Smith's Published Work

PAULINE Smith never enjoyed the striking success of a best-seller. Although *The Little Karoo* short stories and *The Beadle* were both published when Arnold Bennett was still alive, they do not seem to have had the effect of bringing her into any great prominence. From *A.B. . . . 'a minor marginal note,'* the reader gains the impression that the English novelist continued on his path of brilliance and fame while she remained in relative obscurity—just as in the days when she had not yet published anything and he was already the "grand master"! On the other hand, her work seems to have sold steadily. Jonathan Cape first published *The Little Karoo* in 1925. Since then they have issued editions in 1930, 1950, and 1956. The volume has appeared in the United States in 1925 and 1959, and in Canada in 1956. *The Beadle* was first published by Cape in 1926, and reissued in 1929 and 1940. A South African edition under the imprint of A. Balkema appeared in 1957.

This suggests that knowledge of her best work has grown slowly, but steadily. Until the time of her death there was little or no criticism of her work in literary journals, although *The Little Karoo* and *The Beadle* have been on the set-work lists for students of English in two South African universities. Recently, however, there are signs of awakening interest among critics.

Towards the end of 1964, the South African Broadcasting Corporation produced a series of two programmes in which critics and prominent writers commented on her work. The 1960's have also seen a few articles in literary journals.

Some Opinions on Pauline Smith's Published Work

Just before Pauline Smith's death, a presentation was made to her in her country retreat by the writers, Messrs. William Plomer and Roy Macnab. This took the form of an illuminated scroll signed by a number of South African writers. The text read:

We South African writers in English and Afrikaans have felt moved to join our names together in offering you a tribute of our admiration.

We wish to assure you of the respect and affection in which your name and work are held by us and by other South African readers.

We feel that by the delicacy, tenderness and precision with which you have written of South African ways of life you have transcended the barriers of race and language and made essential humanity real.

The signatories included Guy Butler, Jack Cope, Anthony Delius, Elisabeth Eybers, T. J. Haarhoff, Nadine Gordimer, Dan Jacobson, Uys Krige, S. Gertrude Millin, D. J. Opperman, Alan Paton, Daphne Rooke, Francis Carey Slater, Laurens van der Post and A. A. Pienaar (Sangiro). This shows clearly that, long before she began to be noticed by the critics, her influence had been felt by those who were themselves sensitive to the South African situation which she had delineated. Hers was not the kind of success which everybody comes together to acclaim immediately. Her writing had made its mark privately and quietly amongst a number of individuals; and a presentation of this kind is one of the occasions on which the strength of her influence can be gauged.

Opinions on her work by a small selection of South African writers are given below. The list of writers is by no means comprehensive; there are writers of status, possibly with much to say about her, who are not included. Most of them have not commented in any printed form accessible to the researcher; and it is not often possible to contact these persons privately. Consequently the reader should regard what follows as a taste of what the South African literary world feels.

Mr. Alan Paton, author of the well-known novels *Cry the Beloved Country* and *Too Late the Phalarope*, reviewed the Vanguard Press edition of *The Little Karoo* in the *Herald Tribune Book Review* of October 18, 1959. He writes: "Of all our South African writers, none was ever more generally accepted and admired, and excited less controversy and opposition than Pauline Smith." This he attributes to "the purity, strength and tenderness of her work, which excited admiration rather than envy" and to "her own gentle and unassertive nature." Continuing, he says that "in praising her work one praises that which long since and many times has been honoured." In her "firm but delicate art" he is reminded of the American writer Willa Cather. Although Pauline Smith is not Afrikaans, she has produced "one of the most remarkable collections of Afrikaner stories ever written." Mr. Paton comments on the realism and honesty of her art.

She never avoided the harsh and the ugly, nor the fiercest of passions, nor the strange compound of religiousness and lovelessness, nor the despair and melancholy of these lonely Afrikaners who asked nothing and got it. . . . When she writes of love and fortitude and self-sacrifice and mercy, she does not do it to compensate us for the harshness and bitterness of life, but because she sees them too. She weaves them altogether into a tragic and beautiful cloth of life.

Despite her realism, she always preserves decorum and taste, while her tender sensibility takes the crudity out of evil: "Pauline Smith could not write meanly about life and man, because she loved them. . . . She wrote about cruelty, but never cruelly, she wrote about sex, but never sexily." For her, life had to be lived with fortitude. Mr. Paton concludes: "It is a rare genius that is able to look upon life, to know it and to suffer it, to find it beautiful, and to make it so for others."

Mr. Jack Cope, also a prominent novelist and author of the collection of short stories *The Tame Ox*, shares with Pauline Smith the ability to describe landscape and evoke its atmosphere. He writes of her as "a minor master" and feels that time will establish her place as a writer even more securely. He refers in particular to her "sympathy, insight, heart and artistic talent" —qualities which enabled her to achieve short stories like "The Pain" and "Desolation." For him *The Beadle* is not as successful as some of the short stories.

Mr. William Plomer spent several years of his early life in South Africa and has taken an interest in its literature ever since. He is himself the author of stories and a novel (*Turbott*

Wolfe) set in Africa, and provided the preface to Jonathan Cape's 1950 edition of *The Little Karoo* reissued in "The New Travellers' Library." He writes: "I don't think Pauline Smith is coming in for belated attention, but for closer attention. Is she not almost the only writer of imaginative fiction in English who was able to create a truthful and humane and sensitive picture of the old, remote, pastoral Afrikaner life?" He feels that the attention drawn to South Africa recently, for political reasons, "surely has little or nothing to do with any increase in interest in Pauline Smith." Mr. Plomer notes that both H. C. Bosman and Pauline Smith were concerned with remote and bygone Afrikaans communities. In comparing them he comments that Bosman wrote "in a much more masculine way, more political too. And his stories, unlike Pauline Smith's are full of *irony.*"

In April 1945, Bosman himself wrote for *South African Opinion* a review entitled "The Truth of the Veld:—*The Little Karoo* by Pauline Smith." He felt that he could understand readily why she stopped writing at an early age.

Her art of writing a short story is closely akin to the art of writing poetry, and when she had delivered her message, she, like Rimbaud, ceased writing. There is no mystery at all about the reasons for which Pauline Smith laid down her pen. It is easy to understand why she stopped writing. "My spinning is all done."

Bosman's article is highly personal and impressionistic, describing the stories as "stonily descriptive of Afrikaner life on the Karoo" and "shaped after a fashion that a sculptor would understand with his right hand calloused from the hammer." He discerns the importance of love in her writing.

Nearly all of what Pauline Smith has written are love stories. And the lightest love story is laden with frightening things. And Pauline Smith has written her love stories—take "The Sinner" and "The Schoolmaster" as two examples—with a simple intensity that you find in dry, wind-tattered grasses and in poetry.

According to Bosman there are certain limitations to Pauline Smith's art. She "does not rise to the height of that other love and that further knowing, in which stark tragedy has also got its tinsel side and sorrow is the mask for a carnival." What precisely this means is difficult to determine, but perhaps a reading of Bosman's own work will help the reader to understand what he has in mind. He feels that her stories are on a lower plane, but that in her instinctive realisation of her limitations she had been able to create fine work. "Her approach is essentially feminine. Her stories are pure with light and very tenderly told and brave."

Bosman is another of the critics who have discerned the mysterious impression of Afrikaans which the reader gains from the stories. He realises that this is not due to excessive incorporation of Afrikaans words and phrases. "Pauline Smith's stories are written in an English of a purity to which not even Fowler could object." He records how when he was reading the stories he would realise with a start that he had a page of English, and not Afrikaans, in front of him. Finally, the stories "depict South African life with a truth and a beauty which no writer has so far achieved in the short story form written in Afrikaans," and "are all charged with a magnificent finality from which one may not withhold the title of greatness."

Miss Nadine Gordimer, whose reputation as a novelist and short-story writer is high both in Britain and the United States, selects *The Beadle* for special praise. She writes: "This is one of the great novels that should never be allowed to go out of print. It will always be discovered with astonishment and admiration."[1] She points out that the South Africa of which Pauline Smith was writing is, at first glance, unrecognisable to those who are accustomed to the picture of modern times. Yet *The Little Karoo* and *The Beadle* afford an opportunity of seeing what the Afrikaner was like a century ago. It is possible that qualities of character which Pauline Smith depicts in these people can be traced through to this day, enlarged and sometimes distorted into ugliness by power. Miss Gordimer points to the enduring qualities of *The Beadle*.

Like the author's famous "The Little Karoo" stories, this little-known novel has the beauty and authority of insight that reaches out beyond a historical view of life. Even stylistically it transcends the period in which it was written, the period about which it was written, and this decade in which it has now been republished.

She describes its impression upon her in this way:

It is a nineteenth century narrative, without the sermonising; a modern novel with the classic economy but not the "absurd" philosophy of a Camus, the exploration of guilt but not the Catholic refuge of a Greene. The guilt of Aalst Vlokman, the beadle, towards Jacoba and Johanna Steenkamp and their dead sister Klaartje's child, Andrina du Toit, is like a train of gunpowder he tracks helplessly, on the soles of his shoes, through the book. It is acknowledged in the silence of the hard Johanna, the stunted personality of gentle Jacoba, and the ignorance and innocence of the young woman, Andrina, of the destiny to which her mother's passionate nature and her father's failure to accept responsibility for her inevitably led her. When the girl falls in love, one watches fascinated, while she repeats in her own life the pattern—unknown to her—of her beginnings. She loves the young Englishman who has come to the Karoo to play at learning to farm, and plays at loving, too. She comes to grief as she came to be born: through a human being who does not accept the responsibility of human involvement.

Tribute is also given Pauline Smith's skill in characterisation and technique.

Theme and story move along with a most remarkable unity and skill. Without ever resorting to interior monologue, with scarcely any dialogue, Pauline Smith makes the lives of these people surge up through the quiet narrative; when there is an exchange of words between them—sometimes only a bare sentence—a whole situation or turn of events bursts devastatingly upon one's consciousness.

Mr. Lionel Abrahams, a Johannesburg short-story writer and editor of a local literary magazine *The Purple Renoster,* has done much to find publishers for the writings of H. C. Bosman after that author's death. For many years he was a close friend of Bosman; and at one stage received guidance in writing from him. Mr. Abrahams records:

H. C. Bosman gave me Pauline Smith's stories to read when he was tutoring me in literature. I was eighteen and more concerned to reproduce the feeling of admiration he expressed than to see what it was that I was reading. But later when I read *The Beadle* and *Platkops Children* and reread *The Little Karoo* the pleasure they afforded me placed Pauline Smith among the authors I am fondest of.

He feels that of all the South African writers who preceded Bosman, Pauline Smith alone (with the possible exception of W. C. Scully) can be said with confidence to have had an influence upon his work. An important aspect of Pauline Smith's art for Mr. Abrahams is her evocation of poetic and imaginative setting. He refers to *The Beadle* and *The Little Karoo*:

The scenes and atmosphere are vivid but there is something fine and dreamlike about them. The broad Aangenaam Valley is a real, stoney presence, but an essence of remoteness and sadness (which one does feel in the Karoo) is concentrated there. The scene has a breadth and stillness which at once dwarfs the human actions and gives them a special resonance. Such poetry of setting affords me a peculiar satisfaction, and I think it is rare in literature.

Other writing which for him contains similar effects includes the opening of *The Mill on the Floss*, parts of *The Return of the Native*, and *The Story of an African Farm* by Olive Schreiner. Mr. Abrahams also comments on Pauline Smith's tragic vision and the strength of her characterisation:

She writes very tenderly, gently, lovingly of her characters, but some marvellous humility or simplicity keeps her from any coddling or decorating; she does nothing to evade the painful and mortal facts of human existence. She steers near to a sort of romanticism and near to a sort of sentimentality sometimes, but the clean simplicity of her expression saves her. Somewhere between her honesty, simplicity and restraint, I think, lies the elusive but palpable resemblance to Robert Frost.

The Beadle in Mr. Abrahams' opinion "is the most nearly perfect and most beautiful of South African novels in English." He feels that in matter and tone it bears a close resemblance to Tolstoy's *The Cossacks*.

Although there is difference of opinion in the estimates of individual books, the reader can discern a remarkable amount of common ground in these comments. Pauline Smith's "tenderness," "braveness," and "truth" are repeatedly referred to. There is agreement on the strength of her characterisation and the imaginative power of her settings. It is an indication of the originality and inherent value of her vision that what she wrote in isolation and obscurity should slowly but inevitably have to come to win so wide an appreciation.

Notes and References

Chapter One

1. Pauline Smith, *A. B. . . . 'a minor marginal note'* (London: Jonathan Cape, 1933), pp. 12-13. (All page references are given from this edition.)
2. Pauline Smith, "Why and How I became an Author," typescript in the Jagger Library, University of Cape Town. Since published in *English Studies In Africa*, VI, 2 (1963), p. 151 f. (This and following page numbers are from this journal.)
3. *A. B. . . . 'a minor marginal note'*, p. 13.
4. "Why and How I became an Author," pp. 150-51.
5. *A. B. . . . 'a minor marginal note'*, p. 14.
6. *Ibid.*, p.15.
7. *Ibid.*, p. 19.
8. "Why and How I became an Author," p. 152.
9. *A. B. . . . 'a minor marginal note'*, pp. 29-30.
10. "Why and How I became an Author," p. 152.
11. *Ibid.*, p. 151.

Chapter Two

1. *A. B. . . . 'a minor marginal note'*, p. 58.
2. *Ibid.*, p. 64.
3. *Ibid.*, p. 65.
4. *Ibid.*, p. 65.
5. *Ibid.*, p. 81.
6. *Ibid.*, p. 69.
7. *Ibid.*, p. 62.

Chapter Three

1. Pauline Smith, *Platkops Children* (London: Jonathan Cape, 1935), p. 40. (All references are from this edition.)
2. *Ibid.*, p. 127.
3. *Ibid.*, pp. 216-17.

4. *A. B. . . . 'a minor marginal note'*, p. 11.
5. *Ibid.*, p. 19.
6. *Ibid.*, p. 48.
7. *Ibid.*, p. 57.
8. *Ibid.*, p. 59.
9. *Ibid.*, p. 82.
10. *Ibid.*, p. 24.
11. *Ibid.*, p. 24.
12. *Ibid.*, p. 16.
13. *Ibid.*, p. 54.
14. *Ibid.*, p. 53.
15. *Ibid.*, p. 53.
16. *Ibid.*, p. 88.

Chapter Four

1. *A. B. . . . 'a minor marginal note'*, p. 14.
2. *Platkops Children*, p. 17.
3. *Ibid.*, p. 39.
4. *Ibid.*, p. 39.
5. *Ibid.*, pp. 24-25.
6. *Ibid.*, p. 37.
7. *Ibid.*, p. 212.
8. *Ibid.*, p. 17.
9. *Ibid.*, p. 111.
10. *Ibid.*, p. 222.
11. *Ibid.*, p. 77.
12. Pauline Smith, *The South African Journal*, typescript journal in the Jagger Library, University of Cape Town, Section VIII, p. 5. (All section and page numbers given are from this source.)
13. *Platkops Children*, pp. 83-84.
14. *Ibid.*, p. 84.
15. Pauline Smith, *The Beadle* (Cape Town: A. A. Balkema, 1956), p. 118. (All page references are given from this edition.)
16. *Platkops Children*, p. 76.
17. Pauline Smith, *The Little Karoo* (London: Jonathan Cape, 1950), p. 48. (This and following page numbers are from this edition.)
18. *Platkops Children*, p. 11.
19. *Ibid.*
20. *Ibid.*
21. *Ibid.*, p. 12.
22. *Ibid.*, p. 33.

23. *Ibid.*
24. *Ibid.*
25. *Ibid.*, p. 34.
26. *Ibid.*
27. *Ibid.*
28. *Ibid.*
29. *Ibid.*, p. 181.

Chapter Five

1. *The Little Karoo,* p. 26.
2. *Ibid.*, p. 33.
3. *Ibid.*, p. 54.
4. *Ibid.*, p. 55.
5. *Ibid.*, p. 43.
6. *Ibid.*
7. *Ibid.*, p. 42.
8. *Ibid.*
9. *Ibid.*, p. 53.
10. *Ibid.*, p. 48.
11. *Ibid.*, p. 49.
12. *Ibid.*, p. 56.
13. *Ibid.*, p. 59.
14. *Ibid.*, p. 58.
15. *Ibid.*, p. 61.
16. *Ibid.*, p. 62.
17. *Ibid.*, p. 66.
18. *Ibid.*, p. 67.
19. *Ibid.*, p. 77.
20. *Ibid.*, p. 73.
21. *Ibid.*, p. 74.
22. *Ibid.*
23. *Ibid.*, pp. 78-79.
24. *Ibid.*, p. 82.
25. *Ibid.*
26. *Ibid.*, p. 91.
27. *Ibid.*, p. 92.
28. *Ibid.*, p. 95.
29. *Ibid.*, p. 100.
30. *Ibid.*, p. 101.
31. *Ibid.*, p. 103.
32. *Ibid.*, p. 106.
33. *Ibid.*, p. 112.

34. *Ibid.*, p. 115.
35. *Ibid.*
36. *Ibid.*, p. 119.
37. "Why and How I became an Author," p. 151.
38. *The Little Karoo*, p. 126.
39. *Ibid.*, p. 127.

Chapter Six

1. *The Little Karoo*, p. 11.
2. *The Beadle*, p. 8.
3. *Ibid.*, p. 16.
4. *Ibid.*, pp. 177-178.
5. *Ibid.*, p. 23.
6. *Ibid.*
7. *Ibid.*, p. 170.
8. *Ibid.*, p. 8.
9. *Ibid.*, p. 52.
10. *Ibid.*, p. 86.
11. *Ibid.*, p. 87.
12. *Ibid.*, p. 95.
13. *Ibid.*, p. 122.
14. *Ibid.*, p. 123.
15. *Ibid.*
16. *Ibid.*, p. 160.
17. *Ibid.*, p. 124.
18. *Ibid.*, p. 164.
19. *Ibid.*, p. 165.
20. *Ibid.*, p. 203.
21. *Ibid.*, p. 173.
22. *Ibid.*, p. 9.
23. *Ibid.*, p. 133.
24. *Ibid.*, p. 148.
25. *Ibid.*, pp. 182-83.
26. *Ibid.*, p. 197.

Chapter Seven

1. *The Little Karoo*, p. 131.
2. *Ibid.*, p. 133.
3. *Ibid.*, pp. 138-39.
4. *Ibid.*, p. 138.
5. *Ibid.*, p. 135.

6. *Ibid., p.* 141.
7. *Ibid.,* p. 155.
8. *Ibid.*
9. *Ibid.,* p. 162.
10. *Ibid.,* p. 160.
11. *Ibid.,* p. 166.
12. *Ibid.,* p. 172.
13. *Ibid.,* p. 180.
14. *Ibid.,* p. 179.
15. *Ibid.,* p. 183.
16. *Ibid.,* p. 188.
17. *Ibid.*
18. *Ibid.*
19. *Ibid.,* p. 158.
20. *Ibid.,* pp. 176-77.
21. *Ibid.,* p. 167.

Chapter Eight

1. *A. B. . . . 'a minor marginal note',* pp. 65-66.
2. Pauline Smith, "The Last Voyage" typescript in the Jagger Library, University of Cape Town (all page references are from this source), p. 9.
3. "The Last Voyage," p. 2.
4. *Ibid.,* p. 11.
5. *Ibid.,* pp. 11-12.
6. *Ibid.,* p. 12.
7. *Ibid.,* pp. 14-15.
8. *Ibid.,* p. 18.
9. *Ibid.*
10. *Ibid.*
11. *Ibid.,* p. 19.
12. *Ibid.,* p. 21.
13. *Ibid.,* pp. 22-23.
14. *Ibid.,* p. 23.
15. *A. B. . . . 'a minor marginal note',* pp. 65-66.
16. "The Last Voyage," p. 8.
17. *Ibid.,* p. 10.
18. *Ibid.,* p. 9.
19. "The Cart," typescript in the Jagger Library, University of Cape Town (all page references are from this source), p. 2.
20. *Ibid.*
21. *Ibid.,* pp. 4-5.

22. *Ibid.*, p. 5.
23. *Ibid.*, p. 6.
24. *Ibid.*, pp. 2-3.
25. *Ibid.*, p. 13.
26. *Ibid.*, p. 9.
27. *Ibid.*, p. 14.
28. *Ibid.*
29. *Ibid.*, p. 15.
30. *Ibid.*, p. 16.

Chapter Nine

1. *South African Journal,* Section III, pp. 48-49.
2. *Ibid.*, Section I, p. 27.
3. *Ibid.*, Section VIII, pp. 17-18.
4. *Ibid.*, Section X, pp. 24-25.
5. *Ibid.*, Section XV, Sub-section VI, p. 4.
6. *Ibid.*, Section III, p. 19.
7. *Ibid.*, Section XV, Sub-section VI, pp. 18-19.
8. *Ibid.*, p. 19.
9. *Ibid.*, Section XV, Sub-section VI, p. 25.
10. *Ibid.*, Section IV, p. 123.
11. *Ibid.*, Section IV, p. 112.
12. *Ibid.*, Section XIII, p. 37.
13. *Ibid.*, Section IX, pp. 38-39.
14. *Ibid.*, Section VIII, pp. 32-33.
15. *Ibid.*, pp. 29-30.
16. *Ibid.*, Section XV, Sub-section V, pp. 22-23.
17. *Ibid.*, Section V, p. 7.
18. *The Beadle,* p. 15.
19. *Ibid.*
20. *South African Journal,* Section V, p. 11.
21. *Ibid.*, Section V, p. 10.
22. *Ibid.*, Section XV, Sub-section V, p. 10.
23. *Ibid.*, p. 11.
24. *Ibid.*, p. 11.
25. *Ibid.*
26. *Ibid.*, Sub-section VI, p. 2.
27. *Ibid.*, p. 1.
28. *Ibid.*, p. 7.
29. *Ibid.*, pp. 8-9.
30. *Ibid.*, Sub-section VIII, p. 13.
31. *Ibid.*, p. 25.

32. *Ibid.*, p. 26.
33. *Ibid.*, Section II, pp. 137-38.
34. *Ibid.*, p. 160.
35. *Ibid.*, pp. 170-71.
36. *Ibid.*, p. 160.
37. *Ibid.*, pp. 161-62.
38. *Ibid.*, pp. 162-63.
39. *Ibid.*, p. 161.
40. *Ibid.*, pp. 151-52.
41. *Ibid.*, pp. 152-53.
42. *Ibid.*, p. 155.
43. *Ibid.*
44. *South African Journal*, Section XV, Sub-Section VI, pp. 4-5.
45. *Ibid.*
46. *Ibid.*, p. 2.
47. *Ibid.*, Sub-section V, p. 16.
48. *The Little Karoo*, p. 56.
49. *South African Journal*, Section V, p. 35.
50. *Ibid.*, pp. 37-38.
51. *The Litle Karoo*, p. 45.
52. *South African Journal*, Section XVI, pp. 33-34.
53. *Ibid.*, Section XI, p. 40.
54. *Ibid.*, Section III, p. 65.
55. *The Beadle*, p. 19.
56. *Ibid.*
57. *South African Journal*, Section XII, p. 2.
58. *Ibid.*, Section XI, p. 32.

Chapter Ten

1. *The Little Karoo*, p. 20.
2. *The Beadle*, p. 47.
3. *Ibid.*, p. 48.
4. *Ibid.*, p. 19.
5. *Ibid.*
6. *Ibid.*, p. 48.
7. *Ibid.*, pp. 102-3.
8. *Ibid.*, p. 103.
9. *Ibid.*, p. 192.
10. *Ibid.*, p. 123.
11. *Ibid.*, p. 55.
12. See Chapter Nine.
13. *South African Journal*, Section III, p. 19.

Chapter Eleven

1. Charles Eglington, "'Quaintness' in Pauline Smith: Observations on her Style and Dialogue," *English Studies in Africa,* III, 1 (1960), p. 55. (This and following page references are from this source.)
2. *South African Journal,* Section III, p. 37.
3. *Ibid.,* Section III, p. 55.
4. & 5. The originals of these letters were in the possession of the late Dr. Killie Campbell, who lived in Durban, Natal. Dr. Campbell sent copies of these to the Jagger Library at the University of Cape Town, where these quotations were taken.
6. A. B. . . . *'a minor marginal note',* p. 18.
7. Why and How I became an Author," p. 151.
8. *Ibid.*
9. *The Beadle,* pp. 76-77.
10. *Ibid.,* p. 180.
11. *Ibid.,* pp. 180-81.
12. "'Quaintness' in Pauline Smith. . . ," p. 52.
13. *Ibid.,* p. 55.

Chapter Twelve

1. *The Beadle,* p. 19.
2. *Ibid.,* p. 110.
3. *Ibid.,* p. 132.
4. *Ibid.,* p. 203.
5. *Ibid.*
6. In "The New Travellers' Library" Edition, London: Jonathan Cape, 1950.
7. *The Little Karoo,* p. 69.
8. *Ibid.,* p. 72.
9. *The Beadle,* p. 22.
10. *Ibid.,* p. 122.
11. *Ibid.,* p. 109.
12. *Ibid.,* p. 96.
13. *Ibid.*
14. *Ibid.,* p. 14.
15. *Ibid.,* p. 200.
16. *Ibid.*
17. *Ibid.,* p. 68.
18. *Ibid.,* p. 172.

Chapter Thirteen

1. *The Little Karoo*, p. 11.
2. *Matthew* 7:1-2.
3. *The Little Karoo*, p. 127.
4. *A. B. . . . 'a minor marginal note'*, p. 62.
5. "Why and How I became an Author," p. 150.

Chapter Fourteen

1. Olga McDonald Meidner in *The Purple Renoster* (Summer 1963), pp. 38-41.
2. *South African Journal*, Section V, pp. 11-12.
3. W. B. Yeats, "The Second Coming," *The Collected Poems of W. B. Yeats* (London: Macmillan and Co., 1955), p. 211.
4. *Ibid.*
5. *The Beadle*, p. 127.
6. *Ibid.*, p. 128.

Chapter Fifteen

1. S. C. Cronwright-Schreiner, *Life of Olive Schreiner* (London: T. Fisher Unwin Ltd., 1924), p. 235.
2. *The Little Karoo*, p. 155.
3. *The Story of an African Farm* (London and Glasgow: Collins, 1924), pp. 287-88.
4. *Ibid.*, pp. 83-84.
5. *Ibid.*, p. 5.
6. *Ibid.*, p. 15.
7. *Ibid.*, p. 174.
8. *Ibid.*, p. 277.
9. *Ibid.*, p. 150.
10. *Ibid.*, p. 280.
11. *Ibid.*, p. 300.
12. *Ibid.*
13. *South African Journal*, Section XV, Sub-section VI, p. 19.
14. *The Beadle*, p. 55.
15. *Life of Olive Schreiner*, p. 241.
16. *The Letters of Olive Schreiner* (London: T. Fisher Unwin Ltd., 1924), p. 149.
17. *Ibid.*, pp. 268-69.
18. *Collected Poems of Roy Campbell* (London: The Bodley Head, 1949), p. 26.

Chapter Sixteen

1. Herman Charles Bosman, *Cold Stone Jug* (Johannesburg: A.P.B. Bookstore, 1949), p. 28.
2. *Ibid.*, pp. 28-29.
3. *Ibid.*
4. *Ibid.*, p. 233.
5. *Ibid.*, p. 256.
6. Both from *Mafeking Road* (South Africa: Central News Agency, 1957).
7. *Unto Dust* (London: Anthony Blond, 1963), p. 16.
8. *Ibid.*, "Graven Image," p. 81.
9. *Ibid.*, p. 82.
10. *Ibid.*, p. 79.
11. *Mafeking Road*, p. 166.
12. Related in "Yellow Moepels" from *Mafeking Road*.
13. From *The Dream and the Desert* (London: Collins, 1953).
14. *Ibid.*, p. 14.
15. *Ibid.*, p. 35.
16. *Ibid.*, p. 25.
17. *Ibid.*, p. 42.
18. *Ibid.*, p. 195.
19. *Ibid.*, p. 200.
20. Uys Krige, *The Way Out* (Cape Town: Maskew Miller Ltd., 1955. First published London: Collins, 1946), p. 257.
21. Uys Krige, *The Sniper and other One Act Plays* (Cape Town: H.A.U.M., 1962).
22. *Ibid.*, p. 59.
23. *Ibid.*, p. 58.
24. *Ibid.*, p. 88.
25. *Ibid.*, p. 97.
26. *Ibid.*, p. 98.
27. *The Dream and the Desert*, p. 179.
28. *Ibid.*

Chapter Seventeen

1. *New York Times Book Review*, May-June 1963.

Selected Bibliography

PRIMARY SOURCES

1. BOOKS BY PAULINE SMITH, ARRANGED ACCORDING TO DATES OF FIRST PUBLICATION.

The Little Karoo
    London: Jonathan Cape. First published, 1925.
    New York: George H. Doran Co., 1925.
    London: published in "The Travellers' Library" with the addition of "Desolation" and "The Father," Jonathan Cape, 1930.
    London: reissued in "The New Travellers' Library," Jonathan Cape, 1950.
    London: Jonathan Cape, 1956. New edition.
    Toronto: Clarke Irwin and Company Ltd., 1956.
    New York: The Vanguard Press, 1959.

The Beadle
    London: Jonathan Cape. First published, 1926.
    New York: George H. Doran Co., 1927.
    London: published in "The Travellers' Library," Jonathan Cape, 1929.
    London: Jonathan Cape, 1940.
    Cape Town: A. Balkema, 1957.

A. B. . . . 'a minor marginal note'
    London: Jonathan Cape, 1933.

Platkops Children
    (With drawings by Barbara Shaw).
    London: Jonathan Cape, 1935.
    Toronto: Thomas Nelson and Sons, 1935.

2. OTHER SELECTED WRITINGS.

South African Journal 1913-1914.
   Cape Town: typescripts in the Jagger Library, University of
   Cape Town.
   Johannesburg: photographic copy in the Gubbins Collection of
   the Witwatersrand University Library.

"The Cart"
   Cape Town: typescripts in the Jagger Library, University of
   Cape Town.
   Cape Town: published in *The Cape Argus,* December 19th,
   1925.

"The Last Voyage" (written about 1928)
   Cape Town: typescripts in the Jagger Library, University of
   Cape Town.

"Alexander"
   Cape Town: typescripts in the Jagger Library, University of
   Cape Town.
"Why and How I became an Author"
   Cape Town: typescript in the Jagger Library, University of
   Cape Town.
   Johannesburg: *English Studies in Africa* VI, 2 (September
   1963), pp. 150-153.

SECONDARY SOURCES

A. *Articles relating to Pauline Smith.*

EGLINGTON, CHARLES. " 'Quaintness' in Pauline Smith: Observations on
   Her Style and Dialogue," *English Studies in Africa,* III, 1 (March
   1960), 48-56. An investigation into the reasons why Pauline
   Smith's English reminds the reader of Afrikaans idiom and speech
   rhythms.
HARESNAPE, GEOFFREY. "Pauline Smith and Arnold Bennett," *English Studies in Africa,* VI, 2 (September 1963), 144-48. Traces
   the relationship between the authoress and her literary mentor.

[190]

Selected Bibliography

HARESNAPE, GEOFFREY. "Pauline Smith and the Place of Her Inspiration," *English Studies in Africa*, VI, 1 (March 1963), 70-76. A description of Oudtshoorn, Pauline Smith's birthplace, and of the people and customs moulding her.

RAVENSCROFT, ARTHUR. "Pauline Smith," *A Review of English Literature*, IV, 2 (April 1963), 55-67. An essay giving a general outline of the writer's work and background, with comment on her style.

B. *Works by other prominent South African writers chosen for purposes of comparison.*

BOSMAN, HERMAN CHARLES. *A Cask of Jerepigo.* Johannesburg: Central News Agency, 1957. Miscellaneous essays in humorous, sardonic or whimsical vein.

——. *Cold Stone Jug.* South Africa: A. P. B. Bookstore, 1949. An account of the author's experiences in jail after his death sentence had been commuted to a period of hard-labour.

——. *Mafeking Road.* South Africa: Central News Agency, 1947. Humorous, tragic, or sentimental stories set in the Transvaal backveld, most of them narrated by a sagacious farmer, Oom Schalk Lourens. Interesting to compare with Pauline Smith's presentation of rural Afrikaners.

——. *Unto Dust.* London: Anthony Blond, 1963. A miscellany of stories, some from the Oom Schalk Lourens cycle.

CAMPBELL, ROY. *Collected Poems of Roy Campbell.* London: The Bodley Head Press, 1949. Much of the poet's early lyric verse and his satires of South African and British literary life.

CRONWRIGHT-SCHREINER, S. C. *Life of Olive Schreiner.* London: T. Fisher Unwin Ltd., 1924. A biography written by the novelist's husband, an original and passionate character in his own right. Evokes Karoo life with clarity and vigour.

KRIGE, UYS. *The Dream and the Desert.* London: Collins, 1953. Short stories set in South Africa and on the Continent. The author's descriptive and lyrical gifts are displayed.

——. *The Sniper and Other One Act Plays.* Cape Town: H. A. U. M., 1962. War experiences are turned into moving drama, with a strong feeling for individuals.

——. *The Way Out.* Cape Town: Maskew Miller Ltd., 1955. An account of the author's escape from a prisoner-of-war camp in World War II Italy, and of his journey to the Allied lines. Personal, descriptive, and with a strong feeling for the Italian peasantry.

Selected Bibliography

SCHREINER, OLIVE. *The Letters of Olive Schreiner, 1876-1920,* edited by S. C. Cronwright-Schreiner. London: T. Fisher Unwin Ltd., 1924. Olive Schreiner's private letters to her husband, brother, Havelock Ellis and others.

———. *The Story of an African Farm.* London and Glasgow: Collins, 1924. One of the first of the significant South African novels. Set on a Karoo farm, with powerful nature descriptions and moody religious and philosophical reflections. An intense but clumsily planned book.

Index

Index

Hottentot (an indigenous South African people), 125
Huguenots, 103

Idiot, The (Dostoyevsky), 100
Indian, 166
Italian, 166, 167, 169
Italy, 15, 16, 166, 167, 168

Jacob (biblical), 64
Jacobson, Dan, 171
Jehovah, 125
Jesus (see also Christ), 142
Jewish, 54, 55, 60, 69, 78, 104, 111, 168
Johannesburg (South Africa), 11, 175
Joseph (biblical), 121, 154

Kaffir/Kafir (originally applied to African tribes. No longer polite or acceptable), 64, 108, 109, 154, 161, 163
Kalahari Desert (Africa), 75, 162, 163
Karoo (South Africa), 21, 156, 157, 173, 175, 176
Keats, John, 156
Kimberley (South Africa), 113
Knysna (South Africa), 17, 109, 115
Krige, Uys, 158, 164, 165, 166, 167, 169, 171
Kruger, Paul, 163
Kruis River East (Little Karoo farm), 101, 107, 108, 112, 114

Langkloof (South Africa), 40, 102, 103, 105
Leroux, Kitty, 110
Little Karoo (South Africa), 11, 12, 13, 14, 16, 17, 21, 22, 38, 39, 42, 43, 45, 46, 53, 65, 66, 72, 80, 83, 93, 97, 100, 101, 114, 115, 123, 127, 141, 142, 143, 145, 146, 156, 159, 163, 164, 169
London, 30

Mackenzie, Barbara, 147
Macnab, Roy, 39, 171
Madeira, 155
Madonna of the Rocks (da Vinci), 82
Mafeking Road (Bosman), 160
"Makapan's Caves" (Bosman), 163
Marico (South Africa), 160, 161, 162, 163, 164
Marie Marguerite, 23, 30
Maskew Miller (publisher), 23
Mephistopheles, 50
Mill on the Floss, The (Eliot), 176
Millin, Sarah Gertrude, 171
Mill River (Little Karoo farm), 17, 40, 99, 100, 101, 102, 103, 104, 106, 112, 113, 142, 146
Montagu Pass (South Africa), 11
Morris, Julia, 98, 122
Moses (biblical), 58, 62
Mossel Bay (South Africa), 17, 125
Muizenberg (South Africa), 123
Murry, John Middleton, 20

Nain, Widow of, 50
Namaqualand (South Africa), 113
Naples (Italy), 166
Napoleon Bonaparte, 151, 152
Natal (South Africa), 24, 101
Nazi, 169
New Jerusalem, 82
New Testament, The, 65, 121, 130
New Travellers' Library, The, 173

O Henry (Porter, W. S.), 161
O'Kiep (South Africa), 113
Old Testament, The, 12, 14, 17, 98, 108, 127, 129, 130, 137, 169
Old Wives' Tale, The (Bennett), 14
Olifants River (South Africa), 106
Onrust (South Africa), 164, 166
Opperman, D. J., 171
Oudtshoorn (South Africa), 11, 12, 13, 16, 21, 24, 25, 27, 34, 45, 98, 99, 101, 106, 118, 123, 124, 126, 146, 159
Outeniqua Mountains (South Africa), 11, 17, 107

Index